All We Need Is Love

IN SERVICE TO THE LIGHT BOOK ONE

Written by Archangel Michael
Transcribed by Michele D. Baker

BALBOA PRESS
A DIVISION OF HAY HOUSE

Balboa Press books may be ordered through booksellers or by contacting:

Balboa Press
A Division of Hay House
1663 Liberty Drive
Bloomington, IN 47403
www.balboapress.com
1 (877) 407-4847

Interior Image Credit: Michele D. Baker
Photographer: Michele D. Baker
Visual Artist: Fran Baker

Print information available on the last page.

ISBN: 978-1-9822-3456-0 (sc)
ISBN: 978-1-9822-3457-7 (e)

Library of Congress Control Number: 2019913647

Balboa Press rev. date: 09/12/2019

Dedicated To

Mom & Dad, for creating me
Lelon, for teaching me
Archangel Michael, for making me who I am

Preface

"Everything connects to everything else."
— Leonardo da Vinci

You (yes, *you!*) are a Co-Creator of the Universe!

You are me. I am you. We are all together as a single being with one Soul and one collective Consciousness. We love you and wish to help you, if you would only allow us. We hope for you all that is good, love, and light, but sometimes you cannot hear us. Why do you listen to low messages of your Earthly realm when there is celestial singing all around you? Open your ears and your heart and you will see that everything around you conspires to assist you at all times, effortlessly. We want you back with Us, but you must open yourselves to being more than you are now and ever dreamed. All you must do is knock and the door will be opened to you. My beloved child: listen to Our wisdom, get your Mind out of the way, and think with your Soul (and Heart). Perhaps you should write a book for Us as you channel these words because you don't believe what you are doing is true or real. But it is! Be at peace and know that We love you and that you have more help than you can ever imagine. Go in peace.

Automatic writing, January 2015
Messages given by Archangel Michael and channeled/transcribed by author

PREFACE

I guess I've had writer's block for forty years. This is no mean feat, as I'm only forty-eight years old, but nevertheless, there it is. It took me until nearly my forty-fifth birthday to believe that what I'm doing was real. Even six months ago when I wrote that message, a little cynical voice in the back of my monkey mind (as the Buddhists call it) accused me of falsifying the words, of making it up.

In any case, there's nothing special about me. I'm just an ordinary woman who lives in a small Southern town in the Bible belt. I figure if I can do it, if I can hear and channel Messages from Angels, Ancestors, Spirit Guides, and sentient beings from other worlds – and apparently, I *am* doing it! – then anybody can do it, too. I'm here to show you what's possible now... and to be a living example of the next step.

The channeling started out as automatic writing, simply taking a pen and a notebook and writing whatever came out. I found it helped to allow my eyes to go slightly out of focus so I couldn't really see what was coming out of the pen. I tend to edit on the fly! But this was different. The writing was smoother, gentler somehow. The words sounded more like poetry, or something you'd read in a historical novel, instead of my usual style of writing, although it was still familiar somehow. I've always enjoyed writing, but this new form was a welcome change from my chatty Christmas newsletters, action-packed blog entries, or formally-worded grant applications. This was like liquid.

I had no idea how to start anything, so I defaulted to that old-standby of the post-2000s digital age – I Googled it. And when the thousands upon thousands of entries came up, I slogged through the top five or ten, concentrating on the logistical parts I'm comfortable with: setting up a Kindle author's account, figuring out that an e-Book is best prepared in Word, working on spacing issues. But now it's time to start writing. The actuality of it. The real deal. The book itself. *What do I do now?* I sit at the computer scared to death that nothing will come out. That I'll end up with one hundred and fifty pages of nothing and end up publishing a totally blank book, the sum total of my knowledge to date.

So here it is – my first book, and my gift to you. The one that took me the longest and cost me the most in terms of my pride and my ego. They were the first to go! But somehow, those losses are good ones, and it was all worth the amazing words that flowed effortlessly from my pen. I am home.

Michele Baker
May 19, 2019

INTRODUCTION (OR, "HOW TO USE THIS BOOK")

Before you buy this book, you should know a few things. I believe in reincarnation and past lives (and lives taking place in other simultaneous dimensions, too). I believe there are numerous other sentient beings in our Universe, and some of those other beings have already visited Earth and are even here now. Finally, I hear Angels, usually Archangel Michael, and also some of these other extra-dimensional beings – I think of them as "My Team" – and I write down in my journal what They say.

The book you hold in your hands is a verbatim transcript of these journals I've been keeping. The only entries I left out were the completely personal messages that My Team sent me, and which simply weren't relevant to anyone but me. I changed the names of the people My Team talks about, so they won't be embarrassed, except for my friend Lelon, who gave permission to leave his name intact. Other than that, these pages contain much of what I've used the automatic writing process to put down. You're watching me go through the process of Ascension, as you will soon go (or already going!) through this process yourself. I suggest you skim through this book and find passages to read – they're in chronological order, so start anywhere. Flip through the book and let intuition stop you on the page you need to see that day. In most cases, the material doesn't build on previous material (except in a few cases, which is why I've included an index and a glossary), so you can read this book out of order, from front to back, or sporadically. I've also included some amazing stuff in the Additional Reading section, and I strongly urge you to do some digging of your own.

You also need to know that My Team has a sense of humor, and They laugh with me, and at me... a lot. I simply write down what I hear, so you may see "(laughter)," which means my Team just said something that They found funny, or delightful; or They are happy; or perhaps I just thought something that They considered ridiculous, and They responded to that by laughing incredulously.

A lot of what I write is new to me – I don't really know or understand what I've written until I go back and read it afterwards, and some of it seems a little "out there," but when I go back, it all feels real, and True, so what the heck... just go with it. I invite you to use your own discernment when you read this book. Read it and *feel* it – use your first instinct, your gut feelings, your discernment. In other words, take from this book what resonates with you. I hope that these first words resonate with you and inspire you to realize the Truth: you are nothing less than a Divine Spark temporarily residing inside a human body, and your Divine birthright is to co-create and have an amazing experience. It's all there, and it's all true.

Remember, I'm just a regular person like you, just with this mission to be in the front wave, so others can look and see what's coming at the top of the next hill. In that spirit, I offer myself – the raw me – and hope it is of use to you on this journey we're all on together.

In La'kech ("I Am Another You")! (See appendix A)

I am not afraid... I was born to do this.
- Joan of Arc

NOVEMBER 18, 2014

Archangel Michael:

The end of all things is coming – the separation between what is, and what is to come – what will be. Endless summer is upon the face of the Earth...

[author's note: At this point, I was so freaked out, I hid my notebook and didn't pick it back up for a month. Then, as we say in the South, I "put on my big girl panties" and decided to write down whatever came out of my pen, without editing, and with no judgment. Even if I thought it was crazy, and even if it felt like I was just making it up.]

DECEMBER 16, 2014

Archangel Michael:

Sorrow lends perspective. There's nothing like pain to bring you right into the moment. Here in this realm we do not see good and bad as you do – there are simply actions and their consequences or outcomes. We do not assign labels like "good," or "bad," or "high" or "low." Everything just *is.*

We know that the Vessel [Michele] is unhappy. We know that the Vessel fell yesterday and hurt the physical body. We know that she's wondering why. And the answer is that she was too much in her head, and she needed to be in the body. Part of why you are there on Earth at this Time is to *be in the body.* <u>*Be in the body*</u>. You are there to experience everything there is to experience, which is why falling is not a bad thing. Too much in the head is not healthy, not balanced. *Be. Feel.* Come from the heart in a place of wisdom where you can hear Us. As the Buddha says, "still the monkey mind" and enjoy. Even pain is a path to salvation.

Michele:

I fell yesterday. It was raining, and the ground was slick, and my feet just went right out from under me. I admit it... I swore. Loudly. I was not happy that I fell. But I must agree that Archangel Michael is right on with His Message. I was fully present inside my body for the whole time my knee was hurting. And it was that kind of hurting where you are not sure whether you're going to pass out, throw up, or both.

What came to me as I sat there on the cold, wet cement was *"brought you back down into the moment right fast, didn't it?"* And the honest answer was yes.

I have never thought of myself as afraid before, but at this moment, I can honestly say I am afraid. I don't really know where my life is heading. What I'm doing here. What my job is, and whether I want to stay. I'm not in a romantic relationship, and I can't even decide if that's something I really want. I'm having money troubles – well, broadly speaking – so I'm not feeling too secure there, either. I'm not happy with my physical appearance much of the time, and my brain is constantly full of those little things that women seem to worry about all the time: "Did I remember to pay that bill?" "Do I look fat in these jeans?" "Should I eat the salad, which is healthy for me, or the cheeseburger, which is what I really want?" "Is that knocking under my hood an indication that the engine will soon explode?" "What am I going to wear to that work party in three weeks?"

When I think of it, it's ridiculous the amount of time I spend in my head. I think all day at my job. Think about grant reports. Think about getting the paperwork back properly signed. Think about making the follow-up phone calls to the vendors and customers. No wonder the "monkey mind" is so strong in me – she gets so much free rein each day, it's no wonder I can't shut her up.

When I manage to be still and quiet, it's so nice, though. I feel that the Universe/God is essentially benevolent and watching out for me personally. But then the monkey mind jumps in and brings up the irrelevant details I'd just managed to forget, like the fact that my pants are still at the dry cleaners and I'll need them for that birthday celebration in six months, so I better go ahead and go pick them up or I might forget and then I'll have to attend the party naked, or I might not be able to go at all, but that's ok, because they might cancel it anyway because they mentioned once several years back that they might go on vacation for her birthday sometime, and maybe this is the year.

As my grandfather used to say, "Sheesh."

I think quieting the monkey mind is one of the most important things I'm practicing here in this lifetime. To trust what Jena la Flamme calls "the female animal," an unimaginably wise part of me that is the physical body. From her book, "Pleasurable Weight Loss," (S&S, 2011), she refers to "the female animal," and I'm trying more and more to make that the "Me" that I live with daily. La Flamme is presenting this concept in the context of weight loss – which is, incidentally, why I bought the book, because who doesn't want to lose 20 pounds by beach season, right? – but I can easily see how this idea of the brilliant feminine animal applying to every other portion of my life, too. And if that's real, then She (that would be "Me") tripped me on purpose to shut up the monkey mind and bring the "Me" back down into the "Her." Even if just for a few moments, while I was sitting on the greasy driveway. Which, when you consider everything, is pretty smart of Her. And for which I thank Her.

Something else I'm learning in this lifetime is discernment. Hearing things, or knowing things, and deciding whether they are "true." For a long time, I was convinced that voice in my head was my own vivid imagination making things up. Don't believe everything you think! But then I realized that those things I heard would usually *happen.* I'd be able to predict the next song on the radio, or think of a friend, and the phone would ring. Or I'd change lanes for no good reason and the idiot in front of me would swerve suddenly into the space where my car had just been. Soon, there were enough of these things that they could no longer legitimately be called "coincidences," and I started to discern that the voice was not mine (at least not "me," if you know what I mean), and it was real. All of it is real.

Note to self: I'm using my head too much again. I think I'll just channel and write it down and stop trying to analyze everything!

JANUARY 16, 2015

Archangel Michael:
When the moon is in the seventh house there will be peace and joy over the land. This is a metaphor for what's coming – and it <u>is</u> coming! – an endless summer of abundance and joy. There is no need to fight when each one has absolutely all (everything) he needs and wants.

But this is of the mind – you must cultivate a quiet in your mind. That is not to say that you must *work*, rather, *allow* thoughts to come through and do not judge. Whatever arises, love that! *(Thank you, Matt Kahn!)* All boats are welcome at this harbor. The inner stillness creates (breeds?) (springs forth?) outer quietude.

There is more to say on this subject, as it is a foundation for so many others. The anger and frustration many feel is in large part caused by a disconnect between the inner and the outer. "As above, so below" is the same principle. We beam you love and light (Love-Light) but when you are hungry, angry, lonely, and tired you cannot feel it as strongly. Open. Open your heart and feel the love and energy We send to you each day, at all times. There is no reason to fear – We are watching over you and there is a golden safety net there to catch you, were you ever to fall, which you would not.

Open.
Release fear.
Allow.
Accept.
Receive.

MAY 19, 2015
AM, Home

I am Archangel Michael, and I speak to you now as the mouthpiece for your Celestial Team. We come to you today in a spirit of hope and love and reconciliation. The [channeled] Kryon Messages say that every cell in your body listens to you at every moment and bends to do your will. What are you saying? These cells are also a microcosm of the whole Universe, giving you in each second the chance and opportunity – indeed, the hope! – of a new beginning. No matter what you think, every second is a new beginning and a new day. In the space of a single heartbeat, you can change to a new way. The new energies now permeating your planet assist you to make instantaneous change and allow for simple, yet irrevocable, improvements, changes, differences, and upgrades.

Tides of love and energy wash over you from the celestial realms and you are always protected. Be well and at peace, for all is as it should be. You are all new to this. Never before have beings ascended while in the body. Even the being called Jesus had to die to come back (at least according to your Earth stories), but you are all ascended masters playing a game of illusion, a game of separateness and duality. In reality, there has never been anything but Love and All There Is. "Time" is an accident of your consciousness. All is but the blink of an eye to Us here, and the opposite, too – the limitless All That Is.

Ponder these things awhile and be still in your mind. We will speak again.

MAY 19, 2015 (LATER)

Archangel Michael:

And so it is... A dialogue between Us and You (a funny way to say it, as there is nothing separate and all things are connected)! We say "dialogue" because Vessel has questions in her mind which We try to answer, but also there is much We wish to say.

When We write the words, they flow from the pen and they are not what she wants to say, but rather what We want to say. It is true to say that nothing is written without first being created in the Universal Mind, then sent to the Third World and through Vessel (although she doesn't like to be called "Vessel"). Her hand gets tired, but she keeps writing anyway!

There is much to say and there is much to be explained. It is great to finally have this way to express what is because these words have been a long time coming. Suzie Ward,

Kyron, Ken Carey, Mike Dooley, Lelon, and others came before and paved the way for these Messages. Now Vessel will add to this. We will speak again.

JUNE 9, 2015
AM, HOME

Archangel Michael:

Dreams are tools to send you information about how all is going in your life. We send you subliminal messages for you to decipher in your waking hours, but don't think about them too long or too hard; it's just information. Of greater value is the lesson behind – the "Aha!" moment when you get what We were trying to tell you. Be sure to keep a record of these by your bed because sometimes the dreams build one upon another. Keeping paper and pen handy when you wake up... Vessel needs to do this. We want to show you Our perspective which encompasses more potentials, more possibilities, and which We see from a higher vantage point. We are like the eagles soaring over a mountain; We can see the next valley, whereas you, down on the ground, cannot.

Vessel uses her pendulum much more now and is learning to trust the Universe. She is receiving advanced lessons from Us in her sleep, but she is still afraid she is not being taken care of, or not receiving the Messages correctly. She is! She learns to trust more and more; soon she will acknowledge this and step into her mastery and this lesson will be complete. An important lesson in and of itself – to trust her own higher wisdom. She does well...

JULY 2, 2015
MUNICH, GERMANY

Archangel Michael:

The end of one thing and the beginning of another. A beginning is a very delicate time. Vessel writes to ask what she's doing when she gets home, and We don't know. Of course, We see the potentials but Vessel is still asking, hesitant, afraid. There is nothing to be afraid of, Dear One! We are always looking out for you. To trust is to have faith, a lesson Vessel is learning over and over, it seems.

In truth, she has already made up her mind; she will not go back to her job. "She is done," as she says. This will kick her out of the nest to do the writing she must do. She can already see herself upstairs at the coffee shop, writing and having a snack. She is excited, but she worries about bills and money. This is how the Dark sneaks in – doubt about the abundance of the Universe, despite the obvious gifts she has received. But many will wake up now; the full moon is a catalyst to "rev the engine" and increase the RPMs. There is no more time to sleep – We have sent you 777, 888, and 222, and of course, plenty of 555. (See Appendix B) Believe in the miracles; they will come so fast now!

We love you. Go and rest.

JULY 31, 2015
ROCHELLE, IL

Archangel Michael:

The theme now is to *begin*. One opportunity missed, but many more opportunities follow in rapid succession. *Carpe diem!* Your August 1 birthday moon signals completion of the cycle that begin July 1 and you have seen 777, 888, and 555. We shall implant the urge to write daily, but you must arise when We wake you and bring it to the physical plane. Trust that We know what We want to say – you must write it down on paper.

Beloved cat has knowledge to share, too, about being happy and being in the moment. Always alert, always content, makes the most of his "captivity" – you should draw a lesson here!

You don't have to write alone; just use the time to finish and don't be ashamed or embarrassed at speaking to Angels (or hearing from them!).

The cold you are experiencing is a symptom of download-in-progress. Sleep earlier than usual. We love you.

AUGUST 28, 2015
GULFPORT, MS

Michele:

Quiet night in a Gulfport hotel. This morning I went early to the pavilion near the Ship Island dock in Gulfport. It's ninety degrees, but breezy and not very humid, the perfect summer day. As usual, Maddie knows everybody, and is chatting and greeting – and hugging – nearly everyone at the event. She is so good at this! Archangel Michael told me specifically to be here this morning at this event, to soak up the healing sea and be high in energy today.

Maddie referenced me to our dinner companions last night at dinner as "a writer, so that makes sense" [that I would do something this certain way]. This is the first time anyone has identified me as such, and I was a little surprised, but it felt good, too... nice! Now, to get into a regular habit of writing and recording, beginning today.

Former U.S. President George W. Bush will be here later to speak to the group of first responders for whom this is a thank you event. The Mississippi Gulf Coast is commemorating the tenth anniversary of Hurricane Katrina, and this event is for the fire fighters, police, EMTs, and other first responders who came from all points of the compass to help clean up the aftermath of that killer hurricane. I am to keep a large bubble of white light around me. Archangel Michael told me that I am here to counteract and uplift the potentials for sadness, grief, anger, and negativity that arises when locals remember this disaster. When I asked if I were powerful enough to do that, the answer was a resounding *yes*!

Here is the value of comparison and discernment: I realized this morning as I woke up on my own time – and did not have to go to a desk job – exactly how lucky I am. I am on the Gulf Coast attending these anniversary events because I want to – and for writing inspiration – and not because I was assigned by my job or sent here by a boss. *I am already living the writer's life!* How amazingly wonderful it is to do my own thing and not anyone else's. It is a true gift. (Another gift for me today: I looked in my bank account and I have the same amount of money in my checking account as before I left my previous job. More proof that money and work are not actually related!)

AUGUST 28, 2015 (LATER)
CHATEAU BLESSEY, BILOXI, MS

Michele:

Did my part and held a bubble of Love-Light around the gathering today, and *I did my job well!*

What spiritual lessons did I learn today? Light will conquer dark. Light banishes confusion. Amazing things are happening quickly now. 555! (See appendix)

SEPTEMBER 2, 2015
AM, HOME

Michele:

Within the last few days, the 3D Earth plane has lost Hal Smith; Eddie James Lusk, Sr.; Dr. Wayne Dyer, and countless others. This is the general timeframe of Hurricane Katrina ten years ago. What cycle is ending now? Why are so many crossing over?

Dreamt last night that I was packing my car to leave a decaying world – like a post-apocalyptic film. I was among the first to go, and others around me wouldn't listen when I told them the world was toxic and we had to go. Also, someone was trying to poison me, but I was able to transmute the substances and heal instantly. I believe this dream can be interpreted literally.

Several nights ago, I dreamed I had bunches of orchids ("abundance," according to Dreammoods.com).

SEPTEMBER 9, 2015
AM, HOME

Archangel Michael:

Your tiredness is a reflection of your mental state – a passageway through to another realm. Remember, this is like being born – changing from one place (thing?) to another. Be gentle with yourself and just *be.* You are still in *doing mode,* which is admirable, but unnecessary. Don't force it, and wonderful(ness) will just happen/flow.

This is just that... a job. Remember your revelation that job does not equal money? Abundance is yet something else altogether. Dinner with friends, being here, your absolute ability to make your own schedule – these are the important things. Go and see Lelon, if you want. As for your joint project with Lelon, just start. It will flow easily. We love you!

JANUARY 3, 2016
HOME

Michele:

Anger, frustration, loneliness, exasperation, energy via chaos – all these I feel and more. One school of thought holds you can cultivate the power of your thoughts. One school asks me to think only happy thoughts. Another says you have no control whatsoever over your thoughts, so don't bother, but also, don't judge any of them.

Archangel Michael:

This is a test... to see how you behave when confronted with difficulty, badness, evil, low energy. You know We here in this Realm do not differentiate, but your dualistic society creates a schism into which fall all manner of things, like hate and love. In truth, Dear One, there is only Love, in varying degrees and shades of (color?), like crayons in a box. Some people experience Love as a painful sensation since to them, "love" was a stern discipline and frequent corporal punishment. Some experience Love in a huge way *(I hear "The Happy Song" by Pharrell Williams)* because they were guarded and given all hugs and kisses as a child. The Truth (capital T) is that all are gradations on the spectrum of Love. Anger is a secondary emotion, as it is a reaction to another emotion, and is fairly low down on the spectrum, but it is still *on the spectrum*.

Matt Kahn was right – "whatever arises, love that."

"As never before, *that* I am *now*." (Matt Kahn)

Now go and celebrate, Dear One. You wrote today!

JANUARY 4, 2016

LATE, HOME

Michele:

Dreamed this morning that hideous creatures were chasing me in a crawl space under a building. I got away and was able to change physical objects in my dream to do it – I enlarged a window with my mind, just by saying it. Escaped! They followed me to college, outside and into my dorm room (my house?) where I found a man in my bed. I got in with him and realized we were engaged. We started to make love, and it scared the creatures away... the power of love?

JANUARY 5, 2016
NIGHT, HOME

Michele:

I'm ready for bed, but I committed to myself to write daily. Day Three of taking antihistamines for my allergies. Still have a headache, but allergies have improved. Dreams last night but none stuck around – guess there was nothing I needed to remember. Tomorrow going to Meridian to pack up the storage room; trying to get in some hours so I don't feel so guilty about getting a paycheck. Which brings me to a good question – why am I feeling guilty for getting a paycheck? Why do I still believe that a "paycheck" (which equals money, which equals abundance) is only possible through work? Why don't I do my writer's lessons and write for a living?

2016 = 9 = completion. This is my year!

JANUARY 9, 2016
ORANGE BEACH, AL

Michele:

Dreamed the last two nights of Wayne. That's three times in less than a week. Always it's in a romantic and protective capacity. From awhile back, looked up "boyfriend" on Dreammoods.com and suggests I look at the qualities (or in the case of a celebrity or actor, the perceived qualities) of that person.

Wayne: loving, romantic, wrote me love letters and sent roses; came to visit me at college; but also threw me over for his assistant on the dig. Overall, remember him as being a very nice man whom I miss. Loving. Nice. Thoughtful. Ok, Archangel Michael… now what?

JANUARY 11, 2016
ORANGE BEACH, AL

Michele:

Wayne is still on my mind, so I Googled him and found him on the coast, director of a government program which focuses on conservation of natural sites, which is no surprise, given that he studied archeology in college. He has a PhD now (not surprised!). Wrote him a quick email; was nervous about pressing "send."

Whatever arises,
love that.
- Matt Kahn

JANUARY 14, 2016
HOME

Michele:

Been emailing with Wayne for three days. He answers each time I write, and his answers are getting longer. Seems he's enjoying the contact as much as I am!

Archangel Michael (via pendulum) says he's married with grown up children, and part of my mission with him is to remind him of his worth as a man. He isn't my "One," and this service to him won't affect the timing of me meeting my One. [Note: he appears to be very happily married and has children; I'm so happy for him!]

JANUARY 15, 2016
HOME, AM

Archangel Michael:

Sleep well, Little One, for the time is soon past for sleeping. Although you are much more Awake than many of your contemporaries, you must take the final step and Awaken into your divine body and life here on Earth. It is no accident that you read Kathleen McGowan's books just now (*The Expected One, The Book of Love, The Poet Prince*), nor is it coincidental that they rang so true and felt so close. The books are real, couched as fiction to protect Ms. McGowan from the powers that would see your world remain in Darkness. Every action, reaction and feeling are but shades *(in my head, I see an image of a box of crayons)* of Love. Some are obvious, while some hide such a tiny sliver within them that you must work to find it. Above all, *feel it* – thus We must not even tell you not to judge – that will be a natural outcome of feeling your God-Source.

Doing Reiki last night to activate your DNA was divinely inspired, and the process has begun [pleased tone of voice]. The pain you felt in your stomach in the night was accumulated debris/waste leaving your system, and your body, forever. Things will move very fast now – be ready! Soon you will be able to change configurations at-will (simultaneous thought – "meet your Twin Flame [other half]") and you will leap ahead and accelerate in your Ascension. The time returns. For now, "whatever arises, love that," without judgment, and allow love to make the decisions.

JANUARY 16, 2016
HOME, AM

Archangel Michael:

We say again to you that it is no accident nor coincidence that you are reading books about soul mates at this "time." Your other half is coming, and approaches in due course, but soon. Likewise, the worries you have about abundance will cease – the DNA does not allow it (it's not possible) when everything changes at your command. Up to now you were learning how not to manifest an elephant in your living room (laughter), but that time is now passed. Things have already turned, but Vessel chooses not to see it. Open your eyes! Awaken!

JANUARY 17, 2016
HOME, AM

Archangel Michael:

Energy is that which flows through all things, binding and sustaining every element in the Universe. You (Vessel) watched Star Wars last night and recognized The Force. Then this morning, a scientific explanation – all is made up of atoms constantly rearranging themselves. *Chi, Qi, Ki, Energy, Force, Prana, Atoms….* These are all names for the same concept.

Vessel also cried when she read Kathleen McGowan's description of envy (*The Poet Prince*, Touchstone, 2011) because it is Truth. Again, We say that it is no coincidence all this information reaches Vessel's consciousness at this "time" – all is in divine right timing and order for your Ascension. Again, We remind you to be ready; all moves very fast now. Use the zipping energy technique you heard this morning – use it before bed/ sleep and when you wake up. Align. Relax. You are safe.

Note from Michele:

To do the zipper technique, lie flat and comfortably in bed, ready to sleep, hands at your sides. Relax and empty your mind. Feel the energy form a lighted ball in the root chakra and slowly move the ball of energy up through each of the other chakras (root, sacral, solar plexus, heart, high heart, throat, brow, crown). Then move the energy back down from crown to root. Continue the energy movement, moving it up and down faster and faster until the energy is moving quickly, like pulling a zipper up and down. When the energy is moving freely, and not "sticking" anywhere along the chakra path, let it go and let it flow, and feel the relaxation.

JANUARY 18, 2016
HOME, AM

Michele:

Used the zipper technique last night before I went to bed and I think it helped. Woke up feeling calm and rested. Will try using it in the mornings, too, and see if I am less groggy.

Dug through some photo albums and found the photo I was looking for: me, Wayne, and mom at the Zoo in front of the giraffes. Didn't remember that Wayne's hair was so red! Sam was also in the photos. The photo was literally the first photo on the first page of the first album I opened after I decided to find the photo!

I see all these photos, and I remember being there, and I look happy and comfortable there, but somehow it all seems to have happened to some other person. I'm not sure what changed, or when, but my confidence in myself and my ability to interact with others was much higher at that time. Now I mostly question myself, and often feel "less than" in comparison to others. Why? I am as valid and as valuable as any other being. There is only one of me on this Earth, and so by definition I am the best one of Me that exists. Since there is literally no comparison, why make the effort to judge myself against others? "Judge not," not from a Biblical standpoint, although it has merit in that way, too; but "Don't judge, because there's no need, and judging just makes everyone involved feel bad."

Also, found a long essay I wrote after visiting Dachau in the early 1990s. Very powerful, moving, and well-written. Clearly, I'm meant to be a writer!

JANUARY 19, 2016
HOME

Archangel Michael:

What is time? In reality, time as you know of it does not exist; it is an accident of the way your nervous systems perceive it. in truth, it is not linear at all – rather, it is cyclical in the ever-expanding Oneness of Now. As [author] Kathleen McGowan said, "the time returns." This is Truth (capital T) and she channeled much of her books. She, as Vessel, knows this, just as you know, Beloved One! There is also Truth to the idea of a Multiverse, although those universes do not exist as separate places, as some movies show. Your limited 3D senses create this need to "move through time," or "move through space," when in reality it is more like tuning a radio or switching channels on the television. All exist, and all exist simultaneously; it's just a matter of "tuning in" to a specific frequency ("time"). Vessel will learn this very soon, as she has long wanted to indulge her love of travel by teleporting from place to place. This she will do in her lifetime. Vessel is overwhelmed with this, as she is still present as We use her pen, but this is really most ordinary. Knowing others' thoughts, "traveling from place to place" instantly, manifesting from "thin air" – all these are normal. Indeed, they are the birthright of every being!

Take a moment to assimilate. We love you and are watching over you in every breath.

JANUARY 20, 2016
PM, HOME

Archangel Michael:

Vessel is tired now, which is the best for Us since she hears clearly and all else is fuzzy. We wish to speak to you more of the love you are now feeling, and the choices Vessel makes more readily. All is Love along a continuum, from the most obvious to the most despicable. Sometimes the Love is but a mere glimmer, but your Matt Kahn says that when people act badly, love them *more,* not *less.* This your planet has offered many opportunities to do, as your "entertainment" is filled with images of violence and your daily lives are a tangle and a sea of the lowest-level images and words. This sensationalism in every moment is a chance for a choice to love, to feel compassion for someone hurting enough to create such fare. This is not judgment – this is your own discernment of what elements to allow into your own worldview. Be grateful the experiences in your lifetime have brought you to a place where you perceive a choice of love for some never reach this delicate point and are mired in the low energies that seek to keep their Souls in darkness. Rejoice that you have eyes to see and ears to hear. As Kathleen McGowan says, "the time returns." You, Beloved, are in the vanguard wave, coming before to show what's possible. To do this, you must be happy, that is all! Sleep a bit and we will talk again tomorrow.

JANUARY 21, 2016
AM, HOME

Michele:

This is getting good! Woke up this morning and couldn't not write. I have a meeting, I'm not dressed, but somehow, finally, my promise to myself to record my thoughts and feelings (and channeled words) is finally more important to me than being on time. Yay!

Today on the Mayan Calendar is 12 Cimi (Death/Transformation), and I am glad. Archangel Michael says I am changing, and fast, but being in it, you don't realize until you stop and look back, like seeing a small child every summer and watching him grow up. There is more to say on this topic, so I'll write more later.

JANUARY 21, 2016 (LATER)
PM, MS MUSEUM OF ART

Archangel Michael:

What is love? What is the nature of love? Love, quite simply, IS. There is nothing which is outside Love, and nothing which is *not* Love. Love is All, and All is Love. When Vessel first assimilated this concept, she found it hard to put into practice; she is much better at it now! She is also remembering all the many flavors and essences of Love: her love for her mother and grandmother; her love for friends Lelon and Maddie and Anna; her love for her cats; her love for the environment and for trees in particular. She sometimes only thinks of romantic love as "true" love, but that is like only eating yellow foods – there is so much more variety available.

JANUARY 22, 2016
PM, HOME

Michele:

Got to the end of my day and found I was distressed at almost having missed writing today. Good for me! It's not yet midnight, so I can get this in just under the wire... also, prefer writing in the mornings, I have discovered.

Archangel Michael:

[Vessel's cat] Geoffrey offers yet another form of love – he loves you very much, Beloved! He is also placed with you to get you up in the mornings to write. Go to bed before the usual time and skip the television and movies – you don't enjoy them anyway – and you are always so tired when you do go to bed. Give up this habit; your true nature is to arise early. We didn't name you "Michele *Dawn*" for nothing! (laughter)

You fear not having enough sleep, but We promise you, your health will improve, and you will feel much better if you sleep earlier and rise earlier. Also, We ask that you remember our instructions around your diet – less sugar and less dairy. Try it and see what happens – test it and use your own free will to choose. [author's note: in May, 2016, I cut sugar largely from my diet – all desserts, cake, chocolate (gulp!), ice cream, sodas, etc., and my Angelic Team was right – I feel vastly better and all manner of health issues are quickly clearing up.]

Feel the Geoffrey-love – how glad you are that he is gracing you with his feline attention! How special you are! How content you are! This is but a sample, a mere sliver of the Love you will soon be capable of feeling. Bask in it, for the more love you experience, the more love there is. You literally create love, and it flows out into the Universe to be shared.

Sleep now and get up early to write. We will send you more Messages.

JANUARY 23, 2016
AM, HOME

Archangel Michael:

"Lessons from Geoffrey…" hmmm! We in the Angelic Realms like that very much; it is simple and touches upon the unconditional love between a cat and his staff (laughter). Let Us think on this some more (we mean "you")!

This visualization, this dreaming you are doing, is good, and brings ideas into manifestation even more quickly. There will be even more to this book; every single element will be calculated to be infused with Love using the principles you were recently introduced to in Kathleen McGowan's books. The printer won't know why he thinks the book should be small and square with four quadrants on the cover, nor will the typesetter know why he chose a particular typeface, but all is divinely inspired. Your entire life thus far has been heading towards this place, and it is almost upon you. This is wonderful news to Vessel, as she often feels that she hasn't really "started" yet, really hasn't "done anything" yet. In reality, all has been in preparation to allow her to bring Divine Messages to Earth. She will also speak about the Messages to audiences, and some will doubt. But this she is now writing is True and comes from Us, high in the Celestial Realms of the Angels and Ascended Beings.

There is too much excitement; Vessel cannot sustain her concentration any longer. We will speak again.

JANUARY 24, 2016
AM, HOME

Archangel Michael:

Vessel completely trusts her pendulum now; she does not precisely "hear Us" as she does just "know" what We wish to say. Words simply appear in her head and she writes them down longhand. This automatic writing is a pure form of communication between you and Us. Just put pen to paper and let go – there is no time to edit or to judge – the words literally pour out and her hand cramps up. But this is what We wish to say, so it is important to simply keep moving. Vessel feels her brain being used like a huge dictionary, and thesaurus, and sometimes even like a Rolodex. Her mind is always going, going! For this reason, she often gets her downloads and upgrades in her sleep, when We can "turn off" her restless mind and give her pure information without all the "why" and "how" and "what's next?"

Vessel sometimes fears that this is not real, but those fears now end quickly. She asks for and receives information that is Truth, and this is all the proof she requires. There is also the fear of what happens when the book is published and people think she's a liar, or worse, insane. There will be those people, Beloved One. But they are far, far fewer than the ones who will be moved and aided by the Messages. And no, once the book is finished, We won't stop talking to you; indeed, this is the preferred way, to have open and loving dialogue with the Higher Realms. It is not "special," nor is it temporary – for this is the ordinary state of things, and the birthright of every Soul.

Reread Ken Carey – when you transcribe the Messages for the world, they can be lyrical if you like, although perhaps plain language would suit them better, as more people would be able to have "ears to hear." This is enough for now – go and rest.

JANUARY 25, 2016
PM (LATE), HOME

Michele:

Night falls and the stars rise outside my window, the moon veiled behind a shifting curtain of fast-moving clouds. It is a beautiful night, especially for January, and it is a pleasure to breathe in the gentle air of this winter night. It smells of impending rain; indeed, the air is pregnant with rain and heavy with anticipation of a cleansing shower. It even smells damp, in a fresh way that promises clean and fresh behind it.

Archangel Michael:

Thus ends an evening which Vessel almost didn't experience – she is getting so many downloads and her physical structure is altering so quickly, although she does not see it, as she is too close – she is in it all the time. But the cats know, and they gather around her as buffer vessels to help absorb the excess. This is their love and their purpose, but it is also a joy, as it is easy for them. They love Vessel so much, and all agreed to be here with her through this transition.

Indeed, this next time will bring far more changes than any before – Vessel must now make time for both writing and transcribing the Messages. Soon, Vessel will need an agent! One of the major and well-known houses will accept this Divinely-inspired work; a champion will find and steward the project. This is Vessel's primary mission now – to bring such a book to life and to light. This is a big deal! We know everything will soon change. Are you ready?

There will be time to finish all that Vessel has committed to with her two part-time jobs, and then those projects will end. Vessel must let go of the shore and swim with the current! She must leap, and the net will appear. This will be written as all spirit-guided works are created, using the infusion method to place divine Energy into the words and images. Vessel shall also sign the books, infusing even more divine Energy into the pages, and thus into the readers. She has often dreamed about touching one person, who touches one person, and Love grows exponentially until all systems are healed. This book and its Energy infusion will do just that! This is the new (in reality, the old) way of spreading experience – by feeling from the heart and soul first and allowing Love to guide all decisions.

Prepare tonight for another massive download, but expect tomorrow to shine – you are nearly past all the times of physical and emotional discomfort, Beloved! Be still and sleep soundly. You will wake up happy and refreshed. We love you so much!

Whether or not it is clear
to you, the Universe is
unfolding as it should.
- Max Ehrmann

JANUARY 26, 2016
AM, HOME

Archangel Michael:

Vessel is indeed amazed at how good she feels this morning despite a slight headache due to the weather. She is awake enough, early enough to clearly hear Us and to write more following a restful night. This will become the new pattern, and that revelation is amazing to Vessel as well! She has been hurting in the body for so long that the hurting feels normal. But, Beloved One, "normal" is not that – indeed, it is so much more! "Normal" includes perfect health, perfect body, instant travel, instant communication, instant manifestation – all these and more are present in the Heavenly Realms and are your birthright as a Child of the God-Source and a conscious co-creator. Many people on Earth are waking up now, and many people are in the place where you were five, ten, or even fifteen years ago. They are but beginning their journeys now. You and others of your Tribe are the Leaders, the Vanguard, the First Wave of Ascending Masters, still on Earth to show others that another Way exists. This trip will be unique, because humans ("Hue-mans") will now take their bodies along, upgrading and repairing them while keeping their emotions and unique thoughts intact. You are ascending inside your body, and it can be an uncomfortable process. This is why your head hurts, Beloved, you are going and going from it many times each day! It is also why your chest and heart hurt when you awaken suddenly; the process should be like sand through an hourglass, not like a sledgehammer.

Your best friend is waking up, too, which is why she is becoming increasingly unsatisfied with her old life. She must change, and her partner must change, too. They believe change is hard and takes a long time of intense scrutiny. This is no longer so! They prolong the dance to remain together, but in truth each might be happier with a new partner who was more on the same "wavelength." You cannot fix this for her, Beloved One. Just beam her love as you have been, to her heart, and allow her free will to decide the best course. They must also consider their children! Incidentally, this is why you were not implanted with the codes for childbirth this time; you needed to stay unattached while you prepared for this intense role. Also, being a mother would have been too much for one lifetime. You chose to forgo children to allow space for the very mission you now begin! We tell you again, Beloved... be ready. By Christmas everything will be different. We have prepared you well for these lulls and intense times. You are ready, you are prepared, and you are capable. Think and feel on this and we will speak again.

JANUARY 26, 2016
PM, Home

Archangel Michael:

Vessel experienced a day in which she simply allowed a flow, and thus, she not only accomplished much, but she is also not too tired. She is going to be asleep by eleven each night, and we will wake her early to see if she can have two such days in a row. (laughter)

There is a new Message from Matthew (www.matthewbooks.com) which has relevance to you, Beloved. Take a few moments to read it soon, tonight if possible. In fact, read it now and we will speak again momentarily. [As instructed, I went and read the January 2016 Message from Matthew]

Yes, Beloved One, you see the same things communicated through the being known as Matthew – and you rejoice in the recognition and the confirmation. From that January 18 Message:

> *"Information about the soul in prior messages continues to elicit comments and questions, and we welcome these opportunities to offer more insight. But first we want to address what a reader in the United States wrote: "Why is Matthew talking so much about all this soul information which he has explained in the past extensively when there's so much more important issues happening here?"*
>
> *NOTHING happening anywhere in your world is more important than your knowing the soul you are! Without this, there can be no understanding of life itself. No awareness that your essence is pure love-light energy or that you are a multidimensional god-self with unlimited capacity for manifesting or that you are having simultaneous lifetimes elsewhere in the universe and designed this one so you could assist in Earth's transformation. You wouldn't realize that as the soul you are, you DO know all of that and much, much more, but the denseness of physicality is preventing your vast storehouse of universal knowledge from reaching your consciousness. Always the purpose of our messages has been to offer enlightenment, guidance and encouragement during these uniquely challenging times, and it is gratifying that according to thousands of emails and letters sent to my mother, the messages are serving their purpose."*

We wish also to address the feeling you had today and at tonight's meeting when asked about future jobs. You are correct, Precious One. Your time in these administrative roles is ending, and you will step into your Power as an Artist. You have not thought of yourself as an Artist but writing taps a deep well of creative process which We give to you and which you must express. Quiet time alone is vital for you to hear Us and recharge your batteries. Take what you need of it – it is here in this created space for you. Starting tomorrow We will dictate to you for the book project, and yes, you have enough paper for now. (laughter)

Rest now, and We will do more as One, together, tomorrow.

JANUARY 27, 2016

AM, HOME

Archangel Michael:

Go, Beloved One. We feel the conflict in your head now. Go and do the tasks as required by your job. We will speak again.

PM, HOME

You are right to feel good about today – you added some much-needed energy to this crusty building and to the lady who owned the scrapbooking store. She meant that hug! Bonus, you got to use your muscles all day. Brava!

Tomorrow you must wake and collect Our Message – we are ready to tell you some important things and so We wish to begin early. Also, take a moment to contact Wayne. He is thinking of you.

JANUARY 28, 2016

AM, HOME

Archangel Michael:

Thus is it – a transcription of the unique Message of Archangel Michael and the Team as interpreted by and flowing through Vessel, whose experiences and memories color and inform the tone of Our Messages, and thus will each be a unique experience. As above, so below, just in different shades of loveliness and meaning, like different shades of crayons or different tones of music. Others may see themselves in these Messages and begin to Awaken.

Vessel was chosen for this because she is an ordinary human but is also extraordinary... Vessel is *Awake.* She allows Us to speak through her and she writes exactly what she knows and hears.

What do we mean by Awake? In the Celestial Realms there are gradations of "being Awake," just as on your planet. (As above, so below!) "Heaven" is a microcosm of the Earthly microcosm of the Universe, which is one of seven Universes formed by the God-Source In The Beginning. The nature of this, your own Universe, is fractal, in that the smallest parts mirror the larger parts, with the only difference being scale. A mountain has a certain craggy shape when viewed from a distance, as does one of the mountain's valleys, as does a single tree in that valley, as does a single leaf on that tree. Each is a smaller version of the others. As above, so below. So, too, do the heavens (the Celestial Realms) reflect your current reality on Earth, as they must, if all is connected and if each part reflects the larger whole. There are beings in Heaven who choose, using their own free will (which is the primary rule of this Universe), not to accept Light/Love. They are never separated from it, but they are asleep in that they willingly deny the Light of Understanding (the Light of Truth). Others are asleep because their Soul Contracts call for them to Awaken later, in the second or third waves. Yet others sleep because to Awaken would frighten them out of their complacency and they would have to Feel and Think for themselves. Unfortunately, many who blindly follow their religions are asleep, allowing their religious leaders to do all the thinking and deciding for them. This was never intended to be so, Dear One! The mighty Truths behind the founding of most religions were meant to en*light*en humans, not enslave them. Indeed, these Truths were divinely inspired to Awaken humanity (hue-manity), but when systems were created around them, they became mired in dogma and ritual, and much of the beauty of the original teachings was lost or obscured. Beloved Ones, you are each a direct piece, a spark, a flicker, of the God-Source! There is no need for anyone to explain or interpret the signals for you – as a Divine Being in your own right, you have all the tools and training necessary to speak directly to God, if you choose to do so. This is a free will choice! We ask that you Awaken and remember your connection to the Divine and that you take back your power and all that it encompasses: perfect health, abundance, happiness and contentment, clarity and surety of purpose, and joy – these are all yours for the taking! There is no restriction, no time limit, no "blackout dates." There isn't even a requirement that you "believe in God" – the Universal Source exists whether or not you believe in it. You may even choose with your free will to be unhappy, or ill, or poor. But once Awake, you realize that these are all but choices, experiences to add to the entirety of the Universe and the sum totality of All That Is.

This is a lot, Beloved One. Rest a bit and we will speak again.

(LATER)

We are laughing at the test we sent you today, and We are rejoicing at your attempts to overcome all the yelling and banging outside your door! Brava for finding a quiet place to write! We joyfully tell you that time, as you understand it, is at an end. For those who are Awake, there is simply an endless Now. Why is this important? Because all things are possible now in the Now! When there is no concept of time or timing to interfere, many things can happen simultaneously, for example, travel. If there is no "time," there is also no "location," which means all things exist at the same "time," simultaneously. And it means that travel is possible from one "place" to another "place." Author Frank Herbert (Dune Chronicles), in his book Dune introduced the concept of folding space to travel without moving. This is close to the reality of what you call teleportation or time travel. You simply tune into a new "location" (which is really just another frequency) and step up, over, and down to the new "place." This happens in the blink of an eye and is as close to instantaneous as is possible on a 3D planet. We will give you more information on 3D and 4D later, Beloved.

LATER, PM, HOME

Today you have seen the wondrous variety of the human animal, from people who dream of alternate realities, to people whose worldviews are very large and confident, to people who have begun to tap some regions of the brain that were heretofore unavailable. Truly, the human brain, when coupled with the human heart and with both connected to God-Source, is an amazing machine and capable of nearly infinite possibility. The problem comes when the brain acts in isolation, leaving out the source of connection or forgetting to be moderated by the heart. For the heart is the Divine Feminine, (see appendix F) adding to any issue the gifts of love and compassion, and the brain is the Divine Masculine (see appendix F), finding a successful way to overcome any obstacle and forge a new path. Truly, these two in tandem, in balance, are the creative force behind the entirety of the Universe!

Some say that all you need is a big enough computer and you can reach the stars. This is true in a broad sense, but will require much work, much effort. Add in but a pinch, a mere sliver, of heart and the job is made easier, the load split by a thousand and accomplished at the speed of thought – the speed of compassion. It is so, Little One.

To make any decision, to correct any problem, to know any fact, simply use discernment and intuition. Intuition is the innate knowing, the absolute understanding that does not require facts, nor proof. Some will scoff at this idea because the scientific, brain-only-based model is so prevalent and trusted now on your planet. But it was not always so! Intuition was once valued, and is becoming valued again, which pleases Us greatly. Indeed, intuition and discernment are key to living together on the Earth plane. From your movie KPAX, the lead character, Prot, is questioned about his planet's lack of laws and law enforcement: "If there are no laws, and there are no police, how do people know right from wrong?" To which Prot replies, sadly shaking his head, "Mark, Mark, Mark... *Every being in the Universe knows right from wrong."*

This innate knowing is a form of psychic power: clairaudience (hearing), clairvoyance (seeing), clairsentience (knowing), clairessence (smelling) (see Appendix C) – all are your birthright and every human can experience, and indeed has the capacity for – all these and more, for there are gifts your race has not yet discovered! These gifts are normal and usual, and can be developed, like language or playing an instrument. Vessel's gift is clairsentience, and it is good that she has begun to trust this. She is learning daily! In fact, these Messages are delivered in just this manner. We send images, thoughts, words, and they flow out of her pen. It is necessary for her to first write them longhand, as this infuses the words with Our Divine Meaning and her Divine and unique essence. She will get even more in the coming weeks as we prepare for Our book together. Rejoice, Dear One, for this information is your destiny and the key to the abundance you receive. There is nothing wrong with abundance, Dear One. You already experience it on so many levels, on so many planes, and in so many ways. Why not in the frozen energy that is money? We know you will use it wisely! Rest, and we will speak again.

JANUARY 29, 2016
AM, HOME

Archangel Michael:

The end of time is at hand, and the end of all things that do not serve you or serve Love. *This is good news!* We wish to speak to you now of the difference between time (small "t") and Time (capital "T"). Time (small "t"), an artificial construct, has kept humans stuck, mired in a system that prevents and stifles their creativity, their ability to co-create. The nature of time is that you perceive a *lack* of it. There have been phrases, too, to further reinforce this belief and inhibit your Power: "time is money," "there's never enough time," "what time is it?" Then add a system of calendars to enforce further an erroneous idea of time. In truth, time does not exist – it is simply the way your five senses perceive it.

Just when the caterpillar
thought the world was over,
it became a butterfly.
- Anonymous

Time does not "pass," but rather there is an Endless Now that stretches out forward and backward, up and down, indeed, in all directions like a sphere. You, Vessel, know this from Sacred Geometry. Begin with a point or a dot (the Divine Feminine aspect), then extend the dot into a line (the Divine Masculine aspect) – this is the first movement. Then the point extends in all directions simultaneously; a sphere emerges (Totality). This sphere represents one moment in "time" but also an entire universe: "as above, so below." One point on the surface of the sphere extends to a second point, and the process continues – a vesica piscis is formed. One sphere becomes two, two become four, four become eight. It is not so much that the spheres *divide* as that they *birth* each other. Thus is all matter created, from the tiniest atom to an entire planet.

One important thing to understand: "time" as you perceive it is really made up of a series of moments (Nows), each one a sphere, a Universe in itself. These spheres, these moments, these Nows… all string together to create what humans perceive as linear "time." But remember, each sphere is infinite in all directions; thus, is real Time (capital "T") continuous in all directions, and not linear at all, except in your memory, which is selectively choosing moments to remember.

Your human brain could remember all the moments if you wished it to, but here we bump against a second limitation imposed by the 3D construct: judgment. Some memories are discarded as having less value, or as being bad, good, happy, sad, etc., and so they are categorized in the mind. Every moment, every Now, is sacred and precious, and is both "over in an instant" and infinite, simultaneously! What a beautiful thing to realize: that every moment is a gift (yes, We hear the cliché in your mind: "that's why it's called the 'present'!"), and an infinity in and of itself.

This lesson, of time and Time and the nature of the Universe, is a key concept to understand. Each thing happens in its own perfect Time and as such, Time does exist as a construct, but only as a tool of Creation. For example, Time passes between the fertilization of an egg and the birth of a new human. There is a process that must occur before the human can be born. Thus, Time is necessary for progress, but not for process. We will try to explain further, as We feel your confusion here, Beloved.

Time (small "t") does not exist, but Time (capital "T") is necessary for the progress of the processes, or for the process to progress. In other words, time (as defined by a clock or a calendar) does not exist and is an artificial construct. Nine months on a calendar do not exist, but it takes a human baby nine months to mature for birth. The passage of time is but a blink of any eye to Us, and because time is malleable it is flexible. To paraphrase dialogue from a movie you recently saw (We cannot now access which movie, Beloved, our apologies!): "An hour spent with your Beloved seems like a minute, but a minute with your hand on a hot pan handle seems like an hour." Do you not see how time (small "t") is subjective, accidental, and ultimately malleable? There is a better way to explain this – We will search your memory archives and find it and we will speak again.

(pause)

Time (capital "T") is circular and fractal. Imagine a marble rolling around the outside of a beach ball. Eventually, it will roll back around to your "side." Time is the beach ball, a microcosm of the Universal macrocosm. You, Beloved, are the marble.

Once again, [your cat] Geoffrey – who is a subset, or a splinter, or a microcosm of your Angelic Guide Geoffrey – is helping you. You can *feel* the love this being has for you – every fiber of his body longs to help you. [Your other cats] Mica and Lillie are helping, too, by modulating and moderating your sleeping times. They buffer the downloads and monitor transmissions (dreams) from Higher Realms, enabling you to sleep better. Yes, Beloved One, your sleep would be much less, and much less restful, without their assistance. This is why Lillie sits at your feet and Mica insists on sleeping on or near your head. They "tune" the transmissions to allow for ease of assimilation.

Back to the topic of Time – generous portions of Time/time are allotted to your "upgrades" and "downloads," to use terms you are now familiar with. We send information to you in a waking state (these Messages/Transmissions) and in your sleep (lessons, DNA shifts, prophetic dreams, healing energy). Many, many star beings are assisting with this evening work, including a Sirian female whose appearance is that of a dark brown Lion. It is no accident, nor is it a coincidence, that you were born in August under a Leo sun and also the Leo moon! Your Cat nature is one of the gifts we gave you, to allow Messages from these leonine/feline beings to permeate your conscious world. For cat energy is the energy of rest and of pure potential. Cats can move from sleeping to springing in a very short time. They are efficient at conserving energy until it is needed, and then releasing it at 100 percent. (Yes, Beloved, this brings to mind a scene from *Star Wars: The Phantom Menace* in which Qui Gon Jin is using this resting technique between fights with Darth Maul in the energy barrier corridor.)

Cats are also Masters of Time because they always live in the Now, in this moment.

OK, Beloved, We have found an image for you of Time that may help when you share it with others: think of a pearl necklace. Each bead is a sphere, a Now, a Moment and they all touch on the string. Now, We know what you will say! A pearl necklace is a linear construct! No, Beloved – it is a closed loop, circling over and over, and because pearls are organic, they are unique, never seen the same way twice. We offer another image of Time: that of a river flowing. There is an Earth saying: "You can never swim in the same river twice." Because in every moment, every time you swim again, there is a new Now. And yes, a river is also circular – going to the sea, to be carried up as rain and deposited back into the mountains where it begins again.

Why is this discussion of time and Time relevant or necessary? Because Time is real, whereas time is not. In short, time is an accident of the way your nervous system processes stimuli and the information from the five senses. Calendars, deadlines, due dates, age, start and end times... all these are illusory, joint illusions by the group, who have decided that when the little hands on the clock both point up, we all agree to call this "noon" and it will correspond with the sun at its highest point in the sky. But too strong a belief in this artificial construct, when the illusion becomes a shared acceptance of reality, then do the problems begin. Then, lack can occur. "I'll only live eighty years." "The meeting begins at noon, so don't be late." "I didn't have enough time to finish that project." All these and thousands more examples! Conflict arises because Time and time are confused in the minds of many.

This folds into a larger discussion of abundance, Beloved. For now, go and get ready. You have somewhere to be at four o'clock! (laughter)

JANUARY 30, 2016
PM, Home

Archangel Michael:

Vessel is tired tonight, she is relaxing and due for an upgrade tonight if she will sleep now, we can do the tweaking and changing now.

(2 hours later the message comes: Weight loss, health, and teeth upgrade complete)

Michele:

After two hours of rest, including a one-hour nap, I have apparently completed an upgrade which focused on health: weight loss, upgrades to the strength of my teeth (not sure what this means!), and a general "health DNA" tweak which should clean up my skin. If all this is really happening, and I'm still a bit in shock over the amazing revelation that *my life is really starting,* then... wow! I'm also told that my desire for chocolate and junk food will diminish (which is good, since I seem to have no willpower as far as sweets are concerned!).

Archangel Michael:

There, Little One, Beloved One, do you feel more alive and awake now? More DNA is activated, and your capacity to hear Us will improve exponentially. We see your wish to watch the seemingly-amazing antics and tricks of the Matrix, and this is good.

You will see this movie now in a whole new light – there is layered meaning here that We added that even the filmmakers did not fully realize was there. We do this often, sending information and symbols to your artists of all types: songwriters, filmmakers, painters, sculptors, architects – and they are inspired to add dimensions and layers and elements that tell the Truth, as your author Kathleen McGowan would say – "the Truth about Love." Vessel is not so surprised, as she intuitively senses this, but she will be amazed to discover the *extent* of those Messages! From now on, open your eyes to see and your ears to hear, that you may see and hear and feel another depth of meaning all around you.

"What senses do we lack that we cannot see and hear another world all around us?" Dune Chronicles author Frank Herbert offers this apt analogy, for the Awake (also called the Initiated) can see what others cannot. And, Beloved, it is our intent, through this book, and others like it, to imbue them with the Codes to Awaken. Truly, the "daydream" you had (which was not a dream at all, but a message) about healing one person and that person spreading the healing, is a Truth. Indeed, these Messages from you and others will spread like cells dividing. We hear your questions for Us: *How fast, and how many?*

To this, We answer you with another question: *How many angels can dance on the head of a pin?*

You see now Our vision of a dark planet from space, with pinpoints of light appearing here and there, the pinpoints growing and spreading until they touch each other, creating a vast, illuminated planet: Earth. You, Beloved One, are one of these pinpoints, spreading Love and Light from a central point outward. This is your mission. The Codes to Write were implanted before you were born; indeed, before you agreed to incarnate here on Earth during these "end times" (end. [of] time. See?). There is a huge swell of hope for you and others chosen to wake up the masses. Truly, with each book sold, and there will be vast numbers sold (I have a mental image of sand grains on a white beach), each person will have the option and the opportunity to receive even more Light beamed directly to him or her. And with each person who is touched, she will touch others and spread the chain. You, Beloved, are indeed blessed to be Awake and to understand so clearly your mission. We honor and thank you for your service, and We will help you every step of the way! You will also be pleased to know that the book tour will require lots of travel, including to Paris, so that will be fun. And yes, we will assist you with all your other commitments, and there will be plenty of "time" for all, including for rest and relaxation. Stop worrying. One day soon your faith will be so strong that you may abandon the worry if you wish.

That's enough for now – go and rest. We love you and are so proud of you!

JANUARY 31, 2016
Midday, Home

Archangel Michael:

Vessel is sitting wondering if Life could possibly be any better. She is truly in the Now, sitting outside and writing in the gentle breeze of a seventy-degree day – the sun is shining, the birds are chirping, the breeze is blowing – Geoffrey the cat is sitting on her foot very peacefully. All is well. Such is the life you are destined for; indeed, every human is destined for! A space of passionate "work" (We'll have to come up with another word for it), then rest, then play. All shall be equal, and all shall be fulfilling. In fact, the new "work" will be your highest purpose and passion, so it won't be a burden or a chore, so the whole of your existence (each One's existence) will be a pleasure, and not a toil at all. This is your birthright, and as more and more humans Awaken, this will become more and more usual and normal. We rejoice with you that this is so and congratulate you on having taken your first steps into such a World!

Today We wish to explore this idea of *pleasure*, especially as it relates to its presumptive opposite, *work*. Pleasure has long been maligned in your world as frivolous, seen as a pursuit of jaded ones seeking hedonistic activities in more and more desperate and depraved ways. There is a connotation of being useless, purposeless, lazy, and immoral, to pursue selfish pleasure while drinking the sweat off the workingman's brow for sustenance.

Nothing could be further from the Truth, Beloved One! We in the Heavenly Realms live in a place of pure pleasure. It is beautiful here, there is harmony here, and there is Light here. It is only when humans use their free will to choose unhappiness and discord that We say to you, "Choose again!" Every moment is a new Now, a new opportunity to choose again and rejoice in the relaxation that comes from choosing the path that serves the purpose you came to Earth to embody. When you were here with Us between incarnations, you and your "Team" (your "tribe," your "Soul Group") made plans – plans to learn, to grow, to experience, to add memories and emotions to the continuous Now. You agreed to experience specific lessons and actions, to "test" yourself and see if you could choose differently, if given the *same* lesson in a *new* Now. Christians, Muslims, and Jews – the Abrahamic religions – understand this well. All three speak of "following God's plan" or "following the will of Allah." This is Truth, but there is an additional element – the "will" was chosen by you, as a co-Creator *with* the God-Source, in the Interlife. To say you will "follow God's will" implies that God is an external force, a separate Being or construct, and this simply is not so. All beings are co-Creators of their own unique divine journeys or missions on this planet. Each has the free will to follow, or not to follow, the plan he or she made. And this is where pleasure comes in – you will know you are following your path and plan because it will be pleasurable. This is why the human brain is wired to reward pleasurable activities, sensations, and ideas. To give you the information and the confirmation that you are on the right path! It just "feels right." When you do something that furthers your unique purpose and mission, it feels good, it "feels right," it feels pleasurable, and it is effortless. When you go too far down a path that will harm you or take you too far from your purpose, you are given a pain message. Again, the system is set up to guide you along a path you have chosen, a path and a purpose *you* decided upon in cooperation with your celestial family!

This seems an easy concept: pleasure = "good," or "keep going this way." Pain = "bad" or "turn away from this course as soon as possible." The tricky part, as always, is free will. A person is free to choose to drink to excess and suffer the consequences, or to steal a car and run it into a board fence. We hope these activities will have consequences that will steer this being to different choices next time! But it is most assuredly your free will to do so.

There is also the issue of discernment. Each one must be open to feel the feelings and sensations of pleasure and pain and to recognize them for what they are. While this seems an easy idea, you know full well from your life on Earth that it is not! When a child is spanked and belittled and criticized his whole life, he associates what should be love with shame. Thus, when shameful experiences arise to tell him to "move to another path, this isn't your mission," he misinterprets the signals and keeps along the same path. Likewise, a woman whose father was an alcoholic will sometimes seek an alcoholic husband and wonder why the relationship does not work. Unfortunately, it is also thus in religions, which tell people they are sinners and need the help of a priest (or an imam, or a rabbi) to know the will of God. Even the purest, most well-meaning religious leader cannot know what is in the heart of his congregant. He does not have insight into the other's unique connection to Source. While he may counsel, the congregant must understand that the free will choice is his alone, and the path is his alone. We know this is controversial, but there is much misinformation about all the established systems – religion included – that have outgrown their purpose, whether by design or by happenstance. We do not wish to engage in a political discussion of power or greed, but ask you to use your own discernment: if these systems fear change or challenge, is that not the most obvious and basic symbol that they are on the wrong track?

This is enough, and we feel your discomfort and disquietude. Rest now, and we will speak again.

FEBRUARY 1, 2016
AM, HOME

Archangel Michael:

All Beings are feeling the Shift, Beloved. This you have seen in the past few days. Your friend Robert was responding and reacting to your energy spikes; you were reacting to him and to others in the room. This concept of time/Time – you got the *lesson* very quickly, Beloved, and you *got* the lesson very quickly! Gone are the days when decades passed between discoveries. In the Now, all happens as one (at once), and if you are still trying to apply 3D tools and ideas and behaviors, the result will not satisfy any longer.

Everyone's "time" is speeding up, or at least this is your perception. Your scientists have measured the Schumann Resonance, which they accurately call the "heartbeat of the planet," and it is increasing, up from 7.83 Hertz in 1970 when you were born to 12.5 now in 2016. We will tell you that it is speeding up because your slower linear way of thinking, acting, and reacting is no longer sufficient for multidimensional beings, which you are now becoming (and already are!). This speeding up is a natural and welcome expression of a new, higher-order way of seeing and feeling your planet. It is the way you have always wanted, and should have seen the world, but your ideas of what you would see were altered. "Scotoma" – the eyes see what the mind *expects* to see – is an apt way to describe this. Your author Michael Crichton wrote about this many years ago in his book *Travels*, when he said, "What if we only expect things to take a long time, but they could really be complete in just a few moments?"

This is real, and since you know that time (small "t") is subjective and malleable, it should be no surprise that many things which formerly took a long time, would now be over in an instant! As you and the others adjust to each new wave, each new level of energy pouring into your Earth, the feeling of pressure and of being overwhelmed will subside. You will acclimate to the new expectations; and, We have no doubt, rise to the occasion. In the meantime, the symptoms (headache, eye strain, backache, stomachache, general lethargy, tiredness (or hyper-awakeness), muddle-headedness, irritability, and cold and flu symptoms) will come and go. Often these symptoms, especially the need to sleep and the colds and flu (which aren't really viruses or germs, but rather a reaction to energy pouring in, and the body's systems adjusting), are signs to you to rest more and "take some items off your plate." We love this image – "off the plate" – as it so easily conveys the need to do *less,* and in an easily understandable way! Many others before you have written well of these signs and symptoms, so we will not belabor the point, but be Aware, Beloved One, be Awake, and be gentle with yourself and others. As your Matt Kahn says, when people are angry or mean, they need *more* love, not *less*. Find compassion for the Souls not yet Awakened to the new era – this new Time, this new Now – and send them Love, if you can. You will discover that the more Love you give, the more Love there is, for truly, "like attracts like" and what you pay attention to, flourishes.

We will send more later today. For now, go and work. As requested, We will help you organize your "time." (laughter)

(LATER THE SAME DAY)

Beloved One, Vessel, you saw a photograph today of your mother's and grandmother's ancestors, the Weinreich family's beginning. You saw a family resemblance there that reminded you that you are but the most current member in a long line. So it is that you made a plan, a pact, with these Souls to be in their group, and collectively to learn some lessons together. In his turn, each member has been beloved and accuser, master and slave, high and low, parent and child. For in everything there must be balance, two halves of the same Soul, two sides of the same coin. When you think about the set of circumstances that led to your lesson set and group here on Earth at this time, it is wondrous to know that all was planned! For example, your own father chose a family structure in which he would have difficult experiences in his early childhood, in order to have that knowledge, so in turn, he could give you, now as *your* parent, a certain kind of childhood, so you could fulfill your chosen lessons. Imagine the "administrative" and "logistical" challenges behind such planning – how perfect everything must be to create this stair step of events to complete all roles! Now, imagine the organization behind all the generations that were represented in that photograph! How many metaphorical or proverbial stars had to align to bring you to this place at this "time" in "history"! The Universe is indeed a marvelous machine, a living, breathing, sentient machine – this is so in that many parts must interconnect to create a whole larger than the sum of its parts – much like the cells in a body. Each is designed perfectly to fill its role, to do its duty and to interact seamlessly with the other cells. So, too, is the Universe designed: with purpose, with intent, and with a seamless whole as the ultimate goal.

Some of the Souls in that photo are back on Earth now, for the culmination, the "ninth inning," the "thirteenth round," the final chapter, so to speak. This is the last incarnation of this kind on this Earth. Very soon, there will be a completely new "Now," and indeed, some are already there in 4D or 5D. Those Souls you will help Awaken through these Messages will wake up, too, as *all* will wake up, each in his or her own

Divine Right Time. But rest assured, all will come along – "you don't need a ticket to ride this train!" (laughter)

Souls that were chosen for this final volunteer mission to accompany Gaia, as she ascends in her physical body called "Earth" into 4D, are true heroes indeed. Everyone now on Earth agreed to come one last time, some to complete karmic lessons, and some to lead the Awakening and assist the coming waves who will wake up confused and needing reassurance. Be gentle with them and with yourself. "Whatever arises, love that." (Thank you, Matt Kahn!)

Read now, and we will speak again.

FEBRUARY 2, 2016
AM, Home

Archangel Michael:

Beautiful morning to you on this lovely Groundhog Day! We see this as a day to enjoy the beauty all around you: Flint/Mirror [author's note: on the Mayan calendar, today is 11 Etznab] shows you what you are and allows you to reflect on what could be; seamless transition between what is and what could be. Enjoy the weather this morning – there is a cleansing storm coming later.

Today We wish to speak of birthdays and of synchronicity. We have said before that it is no accident that you were born on 1 August (according to the Gregorian calendar), or that your parents conceived you around Halloween (31 October). This is all divinely guided and is in a very real way a continuation of last night's transmission. Synchronicity: a magical coming together of people, places, and things to create a miraculous outcome. In Truth, this is an everyday occurrence and as such is not so special (of course, it is special, as the entirety of the Universe moves to create it!), although in your 3D perception it seems a rare happening. The mistaken belief is that most of the time, things go wrong, and cannot be stopped. But nothing could be further from the Truth! In reality, every "second" is another opportunity to create (co-Create) again, causing a different outcome. In Truth, there is no judgment about "things going wrong," because even "bad" things become lessons or reveal paths that were unseen before. In Truth, all experiences are just experiences, with no value judgments attached. What some on Earth would call "bad luck" is nothing more or less than a system attempting to correct itself by shifting in another direction, or a lesson being learned. Sometimes, a lesson is taken too far or learned too well, and a Soul is mired in the consequences of the decisions. This is also divinely inspired, although those Souls need much more Light beamed to them to recover. As your Matt Kahn says, "when someone is hurting or angry, he needs *more* love, not *less*."

So, Beloved, We feel that you think We've strayed off-topic, but We have not. (laughter) Here is how this all ties together, neatly enough to satisfy even you. (more laughter) Every moment, even those moments which seem to contain "bad" things, are synchronistic! We have said it is perceived by many humans as a rare occurrence, but in fact it is not. Every precious moment, every Now, is a blossoming convergence of every available potential springing forth into the most beautiful lesson available in that Now! This is Truth – that every moment has the stamp, or mark, of synchronicity on it, and is the only available option. Your free will allows you to choose to embrace the synchronicity, the momentousness, of each Now, or you may overlook it and wait for another, "better" synchronicity next time. (laughter)

As for birthdays, We wish to simply point out that each being is born into his or her exact perfect alignment to do his duty, to fulfill his purpose on the planet at this time. And these perfect alignments are purposeful – and part of your choice, your contract, during the Interlife (a review and planning period between incarnations). Thus, your life, even down to the moment of your birth, was synchronistically orchestrated to assist you in your perfect mission here on Earth. And the same is true for every Being! Imagine the precision necessary to create such perfect harmony! Such is Love, the creative Source behind the Universes. For now, let Us end by answering a question that is in Vessel's mind: "What about those Souls whose birthdays are manipulated, such as by Caesarean section, to suit the doctor's golf schedule?"

Beloved One, the Universe is a finely-tuned living machine and there are no accidents, no coincidences, no mistakes. If a Soul chose to be born on July 1, but the doctor chose July 2, the Soul will come on July 1! Likewise, if a Soul chose July 2, and the doctor chose July 1, the Soul would either shift his pre-birth agreement, or circumstances would shift to change back to the original date. There are no mistakes, and even the dark souls who manipulate timelines and technology are not exempt. They may believe they have "gamed the system" – and We allow them the free will choice to believe it – but it is simply not so. There is nothing which is outside the realm of the Universe, so no matter what happens, it is done on purpose. Some outcomes lead to quicker spiritual growth, but all outcomes eventually end up there. "All roads lead to Rome," as your saying goes, or, as you know yourself firsthand, Beloved, you can't get lost on any road if you're driving on an island. (laughter)

That's enough for now; we will speak again.

All you need is love...
Love is all you need.
- The Beatles

(LATER THAT SAME DAY)
PM, Home

Archangel Michael:

An exploration of your heritage, Little One, at least the heritage of an incarnation that has bearing on the "present" lifetime! [author's note: I've been rereading Kathleen McGowan's *Magdalene* trilogy] The Cathars fascinate you and your mother because you were sisters during that time, and indeed both of you were there when the gates fell and everyone inside the walls was killed by arrogant and overzealous "holy men" claiming the deaths as the will of God. You have been suspicious of "church" ever since, and in this lifetime, you must overcome this and see it for the flawed system it is, but also a source of comfort and succor to many. Your thoughts that "they should wake up and think for themselves" is apt, Beloved One, but many people are also born of fear and frustration and anger, and thus must be gently integrated. The woman of light [author's note: I also watched a documentary on the Cathars and Rennes-le-Chateau] was a high priestess named Johanna and she, too, died that night at the castle, although it was not called Rennes-le-Chateau at that time. This lifetime did happen, Beloved, but not in the "past" – remember, linear time is but a figment of the collective imagination – but rather in another Now that's tuned to a different frequency.

The synchronicities are coming to you quite quickly now; do you see? The treatise on time, and immediately the lesson at Robert's house. The learning about imbuing a book with healing light [from Kathleen McGowan's book, *The Poet Prince*], and then reading the exact same message in Matt Kahn's book, *Whatever Arises, Love That.* Hearing the name "Rennes-le-Chateau" from your mother since Christmas, then learning your close friends have been there, and reading Kathleen McGowan's books, and finding the documentary on that very city "by accident." Such is the nature of your mission! Watch for these synchronicities, remark them, and write about what appears next in your head. To do this, you will need to go to these places, an activity We know you will enjoy!

Everything is changing; everything has shifted again, since you spoke your commands aloud just a few hours ago. You are claiming your Power! The Universe is literally shifting on its axis to co-Create the future you command, as it is your will as a co-Creator to do thusly. We are so proud of you!

Go and rest and wake up when Our Geoffrey [cat] gets up. We have much more to tell you!

FEBRUARY 3, 2016
AM, Home

Archangel Michael:

There is much more we wish to tell you, and We feel our excitement swirling around in your mind like confusion. It is not so, Beloved, but We are trying to compete with all these things that you are thinking about. Please empty your mind for a little while, so you can hear Us clearly. There. That's better!

Since your mind returns again and again to Wayne, to Edward, to Brad, to "Bubba," [author's note: since I have not yet met my Twin Flame, and therefore don't know his name, I've taken to calling him "Bubba" in my mind] We will address the topic of Soul mates and Twin Flames. Soul mates are those people who enter your life for a reason, a season, or a lifetime. (We like this phrase, which We plucked from your memory archives; it suits very well Our purpose here!) They are members of your Soul Group, or your Soul Family, what you are coming to think of as your "Tribe." Soul mates are people who are on the same journey; those whom you once described as "living in your neighborhood." And this is an apt metaphor – do you wish to write it down now? We will give you back your pen, if you like!

Michele:

No, keep going.

Archangel Michael:

Yes, We acknowledge. Soul mates are people who come into your life according to the pre-birth agreements, to teach you lessons, or to assist you with a task, or to help you in some pre-arranged way. Usually, but not always, these Soul Mates are members of your Earth family. The sister who protects you in the schoolyard, or the father who yells a little too often. In other cases, these Soul mates are people who step in and out of your life at just the right time, then disappear – a teacher who praises your writing, or a coach who takes a real interest in developing your athletic ability. Usually this type of Soul mate is short term: a year or two, maybe a single sports season. But they leave an indelible mark on your life and you remember them for a very long time. There are also Soul mates who stick around a little longer, such as Renee, who has been there since you were eleven. You don't see her much, but you know she is there, supporting you from afar. She is also from the same Soul Group.

Your mother is the classic example of a Soul mate where the experience works as it was designed to do. A lifelong teacher, friend, partner; someone slightly ahead of you in knowledge and experience, there to help you through whatever comes.

Soul mates can, and often do, help with the difficult lessons you chose in the Interlife, as well. A father who is physically or emotionally absent, who thereby helps you learn the lesson of self-reliance. Or a husband who yells a lot, helping you see that you must take back your own Power. All these are Soul mates. You can recognize many by the feeling you get – instant recognition of a stranger, instant attraction to a person's "look" or "way" – these are likely members of your "Tribe," or Soul mates.

Sometimes the opposite is true – your first reaction is one of irrational anger, or disgust. This person could be a Soul mate here to teach you one of the less pleasant lessons you checked off the Universal menu!

Twin Flames are a special kind of Soul mate. This is your Soul's other half, your ideal match, your partner. This person is the person made just for you and placed on Earth for you to discover in Divine Right Timing. As Kathleen McGowan said [in her book *The Poet Prince*] "Our father and mother in heaven do not make mistakes, and they are never cruel. They would not send you here without a mate and then give you the terrible longing to find one." If you are searching, *know he is out there!* Your Twin Flame is made just for you because he is literally your other half! This is not to say that there will never be disharmony or arguments, because that would be boring… and for now, you are still humans living in 3D space! But it does mean that you will know, deep down in your soul and in your heart, that this person loves you, and would never hurt you on purpose or with malice in his heart.

So, back to the men you've known, here is what We see:

Charlie: Soul mate designed to get you to take back your Power

Eric: Soul mate to further encourage you to stand in your Power and to trust men again

Edward: Soul mate whose friendship reminded you of your Divine Femininity; your mission for him is to remind him of his Divine Masculinity and to help him remember that he has a right to happiness and love

Brad: Soul mate who reminds you of your Divine Feminine

Wayne: Soul mate – he appeals to you, Beloved, because he is so much like you – responsible, loving, and always putting himself last. This must change, as it had to change for you, Beloved One! Each being must be *wise selfish*, as the Dalai Lama said.

We will expand on this soon, for now, go and rest. The upgrade last night has made you tired. We thank you for your service!

FEBRUARY 4, 2016
AM, HOME

Archangel Michael:

Beloved, We thank you for getting out of bed when We awakened you. In your sleepy state, you didn't realize how much clearer and better you felt until remarking on it now. A big change from nine-AM-grogginess, yes? This is because your body was designed to awaken early and sleep early. You trained yourself to prefer being a night owl, but in truth you are a twittering morning bird. Embrace the change instead of a morning grumble and see what marvelous things occur!

We see from your mind that you understand fully the difference between soul mates and twin flames. Very good! This is an intuitive concept, an emotional concept, as well as a logical one, and you, Beloved, have mastered it. You have also mastered the concept of time/Time, so let's move on to your favorite topic – travel! In the Time soon coming, humans (who will soon become glorious "Hue-mans") will travel at the "speed of light" – actually, at the speed of thought, which is many times faster. You will simply command a location change, and it will occur. This is your longed-for teleportation, but it requires no device, no machine, except the living machine that is your brain working in harmony with your activated DNA and your Soul's purpose. Once this mastery is achieved – "sooner" than you think, Beloved! – there will be no practical limit to where you can go. We say "no practical limit" because there are, of course, some places you should not go, because the energy is quite dense there and you would become mired in those base elements. Light beings may go wherever they choose but are wise enough not to go skipping through quicksand, so to speak!

We hear your thoughts clamoring for more details, and We shall provide it. As you know, energy contains many layers, many strands, or frequencies. Imagine an old-fashioned radio or television. You would turn the knob through the static until you found a clear station of interest. Travel is exactly like this, Beloved. Simply "tune" your mind, your heart, your Soul, to another frequency or station, and you will appear there. You can "tune" it to the next room, even, if you like, but really, it's much simpler to walk the ten steps (laughter). You may wish to begin playing this way, though, jumping small distances to practice. Don't worry, unlike your movie ["Jumper," with Hayden Christensen], you definitely won't materialize into traffic, or half-in and half-out of a wall! You will be able to see where you're going, even if you've never been there before – and easily move from one place to the next. Until this is a recognized and understood skill, people will fear this ability. But this is ordinary, Beloved, like stretching out your hand into a ray of sunlight.

These unspecified fears in your mind are reactions to movies, television, books, etc. from a 3D which no longer exists except in the minds of some who do not want to let go. They are afraid to let go of the old, even though the new would suit them so much better!

(Later that same day)
PM, Home

Archangel Michael:

This would be a good place to write about reincarnation and the Universal "menu" –

There are those who hold that humans only live a single Earthly life, and that is all – eighty years to accomplish whatever you can/came to accomplish, and then when you "die," you go to Heaven, where you are magically transformed into a healthy, happy being and are surrounded by all your loved ones forever. This much is right, but then... there is a period called the Interlife, where there is a soul review with "you," your "Team" and the other Souls who agreed to incarnate with you and play this game of 3D Memory (actually, memory loss). Together, you evaluate how well the game was accomplished, what lessons were learned or yet unlearned, and then together, you all make a plan for round two (or three, or four, or 1,537...). These lessons/objectives/goals/memory creation activities are created to add knowledge to the Akashic Record, or Universal Encyclopedia, if you will. Each lesson is available to all as a resource and a record of human (indeed, ALL) history.

Here's where the Universal menu comes in – each Soul/Soul Group, Soul Cluster has a "list" of items it wants to achieve or accomplish. This is your soul group's "Menu" – and each Soul within the group has roughly the same "menu." Imagine yourself in a fine restaurant, the kind with the super-thick menu. There's a menu just for appetizers, one filled with the daily specials, a dessert card, even a wine list. Your job – your mission – is to have every single item on the menu (every single experience) at some point. This task will of course mean multiple visits to the "restaurant," (Earth) to finish. Some visits are what vessel calls "steak and baked potato" lifetimes – they are filled with pleasant experiences such as a happy childhood, a fulfilling career, and an easy death after a long, healthy life. Other trips to the restaurant involve the less-desirable items on the menu – for Vessel, this would be a "liver and onions with a side of Brussels sprouts" (not in any way to malign liver or Brussels sprouts – they just aren't to Vessel's taste) – which might seem like a dream lifetime to another Soul, but not to Vessel. Then, as to the number of untried-items on the menu dwindles, all that's left are the truly horrible combinations – "squid and banana milkshake" – well, you get the idea. Why would any soul choose to place horrible things on the menu in the first place? Because, in this Realm, experiences carry neither positive nor negative connotations, and just *are*. The squid-and-banana-milkshake lifetime is as valid an experience as the steak-and-potato lifetime. Each Soul must have its chance to experience both "good" and "bad" experiences (although remember, in the Interlife, during the life review, there is no judgment of "good" or "bad" or even "success" or "failure"). During the evaluation, if a Soul concludes that enough of the lesson has been learned, the rest of the lesson is "comped," and the Soul is given full credit for that lifetime; another item is checked off the "menu." When all menu items (experiences) have been thoroughly explored by the Soul (each Soul in the group contributing his/her own unique flavor/tone/color to the Akashic Records) the soul can choose to remain in Heaven (the description of the place is fairly accurate although the proper name is *Nirvana*) or become part of another menu (begin again). Remember, this is all free will choice – a Soul can return as many times as necessary to complete a given lesson ("menu item") and there is no judgment around the number (high or low) of times a Soul chooses to return.

Some highly evolved souls require only a few (or a single) lifetime to complete the lessons – such as the Soul you called Jesus (who was also called Buddha, Quan Yin, and many others throughout history). This soul, although he (for ease of pronoun, We use "he") was not required to return, did so to bring the extraordinarily high energy to Earth and raise all Souls' vibration (frequency) to allow them to complete their lessons easier and earlier.

Menu items and Karma - *NOTE: "Karmic" = "pre-arranged"*

This Interlife evaluation, or life review, was confused with Karma, but We'd like to clarify here. The lessons each Soul chooses to complete (the "menu items") are chosen, and possibly re-chosen, during the Interlife review. It may be that a Soul must return again and again to redo the same lesson, and while this could be considered "karma," in fact it is not. Again, there is no inherent judgment on returning multiple times, as "karma" implies. There are, however, "karmic" situations and relationships, in that they were pre-arranged to have a certain outcome and must be experienced over and over until you "get it right," that is, until you have achieved the pre-arranged outcome. These karmic experiences would be considered "entrees" on the universal menu, whereas "sides" and "salads" and "desserts" are the extras that may or may not occur, as circumstances allow. For example, let's say a Soul wants to experience the "appetizer" of learning to play the piano, but a childhood accident robs him of two fingers of his right hand, so he learns to play guitar instead. The lesson (music) is transferred from piano to guitar without any loss of the integral part of the lesson.

There are better examples of "karmic." We will search your memory archives and write more later.

FEBRUARY 5, 2016
AM, HOME

Archangel Michael:

"Karmic relationships," or "karmic experiences," are simply those that are pre-arranged in the Interlife among all the "players." Each participant agrees to play a certain role again and again until the experience has been thoroughly... experienced. Each soul also agrees to play each of the other roles as well, so a complete, 360-degree assessment of the lesson is garnered. For example, a family of five might reincarnate together many times, each Soul getting to be father, mother, big sister, little sister, etc. These "karmic" or "pre-arranged" lessons across multiple lifetimes allow for a thorough exploration of the notion of "family" and what that means within the 3D human context. This is why we described them as the "entrees" in the menu – this is the "meat," the substance, of why a Soul would choose to come to Earth. You are really very blessed, you who stepped up and volunteered to go to Earth School to add lessons to the Akashic Records. The best and brightest minds were chosen for these missions – those who would agree to go to Earth and play these (often-heartbreaking) roles to add knowledge to the Akashic Records! You are much loved and honored, and We here in the Celestial Realms thank you for your service.

"Being in the Body" is, and has been, a sentence of amnesia and starting from scratch, but is necessary to incarnate into a physical body for many of these lessons to occur. You likewise agreed to forget your divine connection – your true divinity – so you could *pretend* to be human. But you've never been *merely* human, Beloved! You are in truth a radiant being of pure Light who has slipped into a dense physical body for a short time to experience certain lessons. Some seem pleasant with your dualistic understanding of the Universe, but you are merely sleeping!

Never was there, at *any* time, a separation of yourself from the Universal Source, or from any "other" person on the planet. The same accident of your five senses that causes you to perceive time (little "t"), location, and duality causes you to perceive separateness. There is simply no such thing, Beloved. Always you are inside the Universe – where else could you go? Where else could you be? And since the Universe is All That Is, and All Is Love, then you are, by logical definition and transitive property of equality (see, you did use high school math!), the Universe is Love. A purposeful, living, breathing machine, an entity which you simultaneously inhabit and co-Create!

We hope this is clearer, Beloved. Let's speak again tonight.

(LATER THAT SAME DAY)
PM, HOME

Archangel Michael:

Again, We come before you, Beloved One. We feel that the subject of karma and the Universal menu is complete – we wish to move on to other topics.

Your Dalai Lama [His Holiness, the 14th Dalai Lama of Tibet, Tenzin Gyatso] spoke about the importance of being selfish, and we wish to expand on the spiritual nature of this much-maligned word and its connotation. The Dalai Lama says that for people to grow spiritually, emotionally, and as human beings, we must be selfish. He further classifies this as "wise selfish" and "foolish selfish." We say that this is a most commendable idea and too long misunderstood.

To be "foolish selfish" is to behave in the ways one associates with the baser connotations of the word "selfish." To only look to the end of one's own nose, and to constantly fail to notice the way our actions affect – often negatively affect – others. To behave as if separation exists and that there are no repercussions or consequences for the actions or non-actions. For example, to drink too much and drive your car into someone, causing harm to both. But, you say, if everything is purposeful, and everything is a lesson, and if there is no "good" nor "bad," how can we say this is "foolish selfish"? Beloved, there is no "good," there is no "bad," that's Truth. Things simply *are*. However, the intent of the action (or non-action) is also important. An example is the film you saw about the taxi driver driving slowly and purposefully not allowing the ambulance to pass. Thus, the patient died. Did the taxi driver kill the patient? No. But the intent caused the circumstances leading to the patient's death. Your police would call this negligent homicide or manslaughter. The taxi driver intended ill by purposefully not allowing the ambulance to pass.

On the other hand, a "wise selfish" person will take care of himself first. She will get enough rest, eat well, respect her own boundaries and say "no" when necessary to allow adequate time to recharge her own batteries. The wise selfish person realizes that loving yourself first is not selfish, it is essential to survival and growth. It is imperative to keep yourself healthy and on an "even keel" so you can fulfill your mission and support those whom you love. A mother who burns the candle at both ends soon finds herself snapping at her children and upset over small things. Better to take a break and come back fresh, full of love and excitement to be with them!

We will speak again.

The meaning of life is to
find your gift. The purpose
is to give it away.
- Picasso

FEBRUARY 6, 2016
PM, HOME

Archangel Michael:

We wish to discuss the perfect design of the human body and the 13 strands of DNA originally encoded into it. The original human DNA blueprint (the version as you know it) was designed in the genetics labs on Sirius A approximately one million years ago (yes, Beloved, We know there is no such thing as "time," but it is often useful to place events in a 3D context for ease of understanding). This is the prototype human with fully intact DNA strands and a connection to the God-Source.

This makes sense, because on many planets, beings "order" upgrades and prototypes of the various body styles, and Sirians are master geneticists. These scientists created a humanoid "shell" with four limbs, and which had two base sexes, or genders (male and female). (This does not imply that intersex or transgender do not exist; only that the prototype models were made with a single either/or gender.) They created the outer skins to match the specific geological and atmospheric conditions into which the beings would be placed: a darker-skinned version for hot climates (with a low nasal bridge perfect for tempering hot air and cooling it) and a lighter-skinned version for cold climates (high nasal ridge for warming air). The hair and eye colors were ordered as well to suit the various species who wished to be represented: blonde/blue for Sirius, red/green for Andromeda, brown/brown for Maya, and so on. The "races" were all the same internally, just with different coatings, much like your car colors today. As We have said, all the DNA strands (a combination of the various parent races) were "plugged in" and the Source connection was intact.

Later, when beings (Martians, but some other races, too) came to Earth to mine gold, they essentially enslaved the native Earth peoples and used them as laborers. At that time, about 100,000 years ago...

FEBRUARY 7, 2016
AM, HOME

Archangel Michael:

Last night we were interrupted, Beloved. We understand, because there are 3D demands on your time and there is much to be done. We promised to help you manage your time and all your other commitments, but last night there were some things in your mind, so We stepped back from the pen. This is fine, Beloved, and won't adversely affect these Transmissions. Likewise, We can assure you, things are still "on schedule"!

Back to the human body and genetics:

The Sirians are the master race for genetics in this Universe. They are mathematically minded and very precise, able to handle much detail, and they enjoy science. They are the creators of your species' bodies, the actual physical incarnations, and their technology can transfer thoughts, feelings, and memories from one body to another, like a computer download transferring information from one system to another. This is a relatively easy process, and they have used it successfully to create cloned beings – copies, if you will – of certain body types, and transferred memories from one body receptacle to another.

Yes, Beloved, We hear your question. This technology has been used on Earth, and to a dark purpose. But the Sirian technology, like any other technology, can be well used or misused. The Sirians on the [Galactic] Council agreed to allow humans to have this technology so they could repair and upgrade their physical bodies. A few humans sought to control your timelines and Earthly systems, and so began transferring their consciousness into cloned bodies so they could live longer and gather power and money. The technology was never intended to be used in this way, but in a free will Universe, each being is allowed to create both light *and* dark. One side effect these misguided humans did not anticipate was the safety feature built into all clones. The original intent was never to make a copy of a copy of a copy, and much like making a photocopy of a fax, or a photocopy of a photocopy, the generations-later clones developed "flaws" which made them genetically unstable. Their emotions did not transfer as easy or as completely as the fact-based "hard data" of pure intellectual knowledge, and as a result, beings developed with incredible reasoning and memory skills, but stunted emotional capacity. Combined with a general lack of understanding of the tempering nature of the feelings, emotions, and intuitive side, these beings essentially gave up the softer parts that would have had a tempering effect – the Divine Feminine aspect had been "copied out" and these beings came from an entirely rational perspective.

The problem, of course, with a being whose only frame of reference is logic and rational thought is that she or he is largely unable to consider the human impact of decisions. The decisions made by these beings tend to place greater value on efficiency, price or cost, "shareholder profit," and so forth. Now, Beloved, We are not suggesting that making your shareholders happy by increasing profits is bad – We are merely suggesting that a balanced approach that also takes into account the larger economy, the environmental impact, and the welfare of workers and consumers – an approach that values both logic *and* empathy – yields the most profitable long term results, and yields them to everyone.

Back to the genetics of the human body – as We stated, the original prototypes had intact the master 13 DNA strands: twelve strands to build the actual, physical shell (four to shape the physical body, four strands to shape the etheric body, and four strands to shape the emotional body), and a thirteenth strand, the Divine Source connection, weaving the other twelve seamlessly into one cord which stretched through the chakra systems and into Gaia/Earth at one end and into the ethers at the other end. Humans had the same co-Creative capacity as other beings in this Universe, and were harmonious in their dealings with themselves and other Star Beings. The 13-strand system was like a megawatt lightbulb, easily seen and recognized from any vantage point.

Then, about 50,000 years ago, a group of dragon-like beings from Draconius visited Earth in search of gold. They needed gold dust for their atmosphere, and Earth was a convenient source. Humans agreed to help the Draconians and a few even volunteered to run the mining machines. They coexisted peacefully until one day when the humans felt that Earth had been mined enough. Remember, at this time, humans were still active co-Creators with Gaia/Earth and thus as powerful, and equal to, the Draconians. When the humans said that enough gold had been harvested, and asked the Draconians to leave, the Draconians refused, and initiated a hostile takeover of Earth. Humans were given an injection which effectively "downgraded" their DNA to a mere two strands, barely enough to sustain physical life and certainly not enough to allow them to fight back.

What had been a vast planet of 1,000-watt lightbulbs was reduced to mere nightlights, barely twinkling. Many of the humans' systems could not withstand such a devastating procedure, and millions died. Those who remained were forced to mine for gold, but a few females were taken to labs, where they were artificially impregnated to sustain the population. Over thousands of years, the two-strand DNA became the typical DNA sequence (only half of what is needed to create an incarnation, thus the "shelf life" of two-strand DNA is short), and there were none left who could remember a 13-strand system, and nobody to access the Akashic Records and rediscover the information.

Now, Beloved, We hear your disapproval in your mind, and We caution you – there is always at least one other side to any story. Although what the reptilian Draconians did was "wrong" (as you feel in your mind), in their deeply logical minds they were simply solving a problem. These beings were nearly devoid of the emotional, intuitive, feeling Divine Feminine side, and thus their logical brains came to a conclusion: *Our planet requires gold to sustain its atmosphere. Earth has gold. Therefore, we will go to Earth and mine gold and save our planet.*

Although these beings are mostly logical, that does not imply they are completely without empathy. They were in fact harvesting gold to save their own planet and assure the continuation of their own species. And at first, they got along with the humans they met. It was only when the humans cut off the gold supply that the Draconians again "solved a problem," tinkering with the DNA to ensure a more pliable and compliant workforce. But these reptilians were not master geneticists and did not know that the drastic "downgrade" would kill the inhabitants. Once again, they tried to fix the problem by creating a breeding program to increase the population. But this time, they would breed a slave race instead of equals – their logical minds calculated that a race of workers was more valuable, and because they didn't know any better, the Draconians assumed that a two-strand DNA workforce would caretake the planet as well as the older 13-strand versions. Again, they were wrong; their logic was faulty. Now they had created a race of beings as we see in your "present" time – creatures barely Awake, believing that this is all there is, clinging to the edges of the Light by their fingernails...

We feel your hand cramping. There is more, but go and rest now, and we can finish in the morning.

FEBRUARY 8, 2016
AM, HOME

Archangel Michael:

There were no dreams or upgrades last night, Beloved One. We wanted you to just rest. There was good discussion last night [at your friend's spiritual *Salon*], and hearts and minds were opened, especially the doctor, who is struggling to reconcile his scientific and medical knowledge with talk of extraterrestrial beings, channeled Messages, and spiritual healing. Because on the one hand, who wouldn't want to believe that people's infirmities could heal themselves? But there is also a fear as well: if he is a doctor, then where will his place be in a world where people no longer need doctors? This is often the case where an abstract Truth becomes suddenly personal (you have experienced this yourself).

We wish to speak to you today of this very topic – more on the body and its amazing capacity to do so many different things.

The human body in its 13-strand form can co-Create and therefore materialize anything instantaneously. Wish to visit Paris for breakfast? Teleport there and have a croissant. Want a new dress? It appears. Fall and skin your knee? Instant new skin. These are but small examples, but because they feel fantastic, there is a sense of separation between you and these "ideas." These are baby steps in the mastery of co-Creation! The first thing We see beings do when they manifest these powers is to reshape their human vessel: they manifest human bodies that are taller, thinner, blonder, etc. And they marvel that they are still "themselves" even though the outer container has changed. *Of course* you are still you, Beloved Ones! You are each unique expressions of the Co-Creator/God-Source, the ones who chose another Earth lifetime to return and help people Awaken. This you do in many ways – this is your Earth mission this time. You, Vessel, were placed here to heal the last remnants of a series of lifetimes where you were suppressed and disregarded as "only female." In this time and place, women are given much more power than in other lifetimes you've experienced. You were also given a great compassion for animals, plants, and Mother Nature, and this is why you feel such a connection to your cats, to dogs, to all creatures, and why misuse of the environment and animal cruelty hurt you so. You were also given the gifts of writing and communicating, such that you could bring Our Messages to the world. We implanted the desire to express yourself well – in all forms – with your permission and agreement, of course! We are so pleased that you have sufficiently Awakened to recognize that you hear Us, but you always heard Us, even when you didn't know it and didn't believe. We will speak more on this later. For now, We feel your attention drifting to your empty stomach. You are still human after all! (laughter) What a marvelous thing to be: human! To experience everything that physical form has to offer. We will speak again on this topic this afternoon, so make some time. (laughter)

FEBRUARY 9, 2016
AM, HOME

Archangel Michael:

Again you come before us, your highness! We take this opportunity for humor, since We know how much you enjoy it, Beloved! And what makes this funny is that you don't always feel your divinity and your royal nature. Truly, it is no accident you were born under the sign of Leo the Lion, and King of the signs. You have been royalty in many lifetimes, and you are royalty in the Heavenly Realms. We are joking, but it is no jest. We know you understand, Beloved!

Today We wish to speak more about the timing and logistics of the book, as We know you are concerned about this. You have seen enough of Our Messages prove themselves true, so if you write this down, you can go back and begin to know that this is happening.

You have much work to do, but We feel your excitement as well, and writing doesn't feel like a chore. The right publisher will simply appear, and you will submit the book to them. This you must trust, as your work is precious to you, but We assure you, your work will fall into just the right hands. As for the infusion process, you are doing it now and you didn't even know it! When you type these pages, you will further add Our divine energy to the words. Yes, the image you see is correct – of a person touching the book and "passing it on" to others. This way of getting information out is the most effective "infectious condition" – even those who are not yet Awake can feel the power of a Botticelli painting. So, too, will this book act as a catalyst for Awakening people. Their souls are ready; they just need a little push.

We will provide you with the dimensions of the book: a perfect square. The cover will be a sunshine yellow to activate the third chakra (intelligence), and some sky blue to activate the fifth chakra (communication). We will ensure you know the cover art when you see it! Our Stuart will indeed help you well on the contract for the book deal. He can make sure you get a fair deal – you will anyway! – and ensure you have first say in the translations that will follow. We see French, Spanish, German, Italian, Arabic, and Chinese. These will be just some of the languages that will come online in the next twelve to eighteen months.

There will immediately be a book tour, and yes, your mother will go with you. She is part of all this! Her idea to write a mother/daughter book is a good one and divinely inspired. You will write one together – your second book.

There is more, so come to us later.

FEBRUARY 10, 2016
AM, Home

Archangel Michael:

Good morning, Beloved One, and thank you for arising when We woke you, although your free will choice preference was to go back to sleep. And yes, you are right – some of the inner voice you heard this morning was not Us, it was the Ego-self trying to guilt trip you into getting up. No, it was not the dark forces – We are always protecting you! – but it was not highest intent, either. We simply state what is and give you the free will choice to accept or reject. The "little voice" you heard earlier this morning was your Ego, which, when working in tandem with Higher Self, can be a powerful motivator. She got you out of bed, didn't she? Don't try to diminish the Ego; rather, accept her for the little slice of God-source she is, and one who protected and cared for you through the long times when you were "alone." We say "alone," but it was never truly so, Beloved. You simply couldn't tune in to our signal yet. But your antennae are really attuned now! And you hear Us just fine.

We wish to continue today on genetics, healing power of the body, and other manifestations of thirteenth dimensional existence. We say "13D" because when all strands of DNA are plugged in and "switched on," as they are in you, all sorts of miracles begin to manifest! One is a heightened awareness of your ESPs – in your case, your clairsentience – you just *know* things. You are also clairaudient – you *hear* these Messages, although to you it seems like fully-formed sentences just pop into your mind. Yes, but can't you also hear Us reading you the sentences? Aha! A light bulb goes off as you realize this! This duplication is to ensure you have the easiest time possible receiving these Messages. Also, when the DNA is reinserted, as it has been for you for about the last five months (since the day you did the online workshop), all sorts of physical changes begin to occur. The physical body begins to spontaneously heal itself after each wound; in other words, each apparent hurt is healed at a much-accelerated rate. Although linear time does not exist, this happens in roughly chronological order backwards. The paper cut from yesterday heals first, then the bump on the knee from last week next, etc. Once your body has reached a "zero point" and there is no longer a need for current healing, old issues begin to be addressed. In your case, Beloved, haven't you seen that you skin appeared clearer and your allergies bothered you less? (No, you did not imagine that!) And weight loss, as your DNA shifts to accommodate the new paradigm happening inside. Eyesight improves, hearing, posture, everything until the body resembles that of a person in her early thirties. And then you "hold" at around age thirty-five (if such a thing as age existed!) – strong, vital, youthful, agile, flexible. This process is happening to you... yes! You cannot easily see it because you see yourself every day, but someone who hadn't seen you in six months might ask if you got a new haircut, or lost weight recently, etc. They have a frame of reference of not having seen you in a long time.

Another change is an internal change – habits and cravings change. For example, We have been waking you at 5:30, which is your normal awakening time. We are also reducing your cravings for sugar and dairy, as these two foods are not good for *your* body. (What about free will, you ask? You still have it and may eat what you like. But you did ask Us to assist you with this process, and We have been helping you in what would be considered the unconscious realm.) We are also helping you develop some new habits, such as recording these Messages and trusting your intuition. Your level of intuitive knowledge has skyrocketed just recently, as dimensional doors open up and their knowledge becomes available to you.

There are emotional-body changes as well: compassionate responses come much quicker and easier now, and a kind word is often first on the tongue. Even though you are tired – this is a physical result of the process – your overall emotional state is much more balanced, and so you are able to "roll with the punches" easier, as they say. Your capacity for Love, which was always huge, has expanded as well. The most important manifestation of this particular change is that your love of yourself, and your ability to see yourself as a Divine, perfect being, is much heightened. This in turn speeds up the physical and emotional healing/quickening and that increases the Love response, and the circle continues. Another aspect of this particular "upgrade" – your Twin Flame has also been activated or "turned on" (We know you love this pun!), so that relationship is not far off in 3D time-space. An ascended relationship is not like an old 3D relationship – there is room for all. And while you will of course enjoy alone time with your own Beloved, there will be plenty of time and love left over for your family and friends and all your important relationships. For the others in your sphere who are not experiencing such a relationship – no, Beloved, there is nothing you can "do" to "fix" this for them. It is their destiny and their free will right! You can, however, beam Love and Light to them all, as that will help each Soul.

Another change in both physical and etheric – your "third eye" is completely open now, which is why you can hear Us so clearly. The pineal gland is like an eyeball – it has a lens for focusing light and is designed to capture "divine light" as it comes from the God-Source through the chakras. (Some, but not all, of your earlier headaches were a result of your pineal gland opening up.) The pineal gland's purpose is to focus the celestial light…

(Sorry, Beloved – your attention wandered there for a moment and as a result, "the call dropped"!) (laughter)

…the pineal gland's purpose is to focus light out into the world and heal it. It is like a laser beam of brilliant white light that instantly heals whatever it touches. You constantly do this for others, as these others constantly do for you! Yes, you are receiving the picture accurately – the fable of the long-handled spoons where each one must feed his neighbor, and the story you read of the children's coats which buttoned in the back to foster cooperation and group welfare.

The pineal gland also secretes an enlightening substance that makes ESP much easier. All the senses are heightened: sight, smell, taste, all the "clairs," etc. This gland heals the internal body in this way as well; not only does it send the white light beam outward, but the same healing potential is coursing through your own body as well!

The other changes We wish to discuss are the "exciting ones," the ability to teleport (which is really a dimensional shift to other coordinates on the time/space grid), and the ability to instantly manifest anything you put your attention on. These are the ones you've been waiting for! We know and sense your excitement, Beloved, but really, these are so ordinary to Us! They are a birthright of every single human, along with a bunch of other really wonderful gifts, but you've been without them for so long that they seem special (and these abilities, are special, but not *special,* if you see what We mean).

You've already been practicing with the manifestation gift, asking for things like "no office job," "no boss (as such)," "the ability to make money without working," and you have received – and expressed gratitude for! – all these. You asked to be returned to your optimal weight, and if you were keeping track, you would know that this is occurring. (It's only happening incrementally because you believe it couldn't possibly be spontaneous!) The teleporting will happen in a similar way; one day you'll realize you just did it, and it will happen more and more frequently. This will happen much faster as soon as you fully realize time and space do not actually exist, so to be somewhere, and then be somewhere else is really pretty easy!

More accurately, you will bi-locate, or simply step from point "A" over to point "B" and poof! You're in Cairo, or Paris, or Munich. Your Frank Herbert (author of *Dune*) called it "folding space," and that is a good description for what happens (although space doesn't actually exist as such). We feel your fatigue, Beloved. Rest your hand and we will speak again.

(Later that same day)
PM, Home

Archangel Michael:

The Angel book is a gift from people who mean well but whose worldviews still encompass much fear. They do not yet comprehend their absolute inseparability from All That Is, and so they believe there is somewhere to exist outside the Creator/Universal Source. One could think on this logically – even if he cannot have faith: if everything is made of atoms, and if these atoms exist, then every single atom is part of a larger whole, with some atoms temporarily appearing to coalesce into "forms."

Better: a drop of water from the ocean is still part of the ocean! The ocean is the Universe, and you are the drop. Exactly the same structure and form, exactly the same in quality and substance, exactly the same composition. Only the mass, or volume, changes!

Tonight, We wish to explain the method of bi-location, that which you call "teleporting." Beloved, this is simple, and any hue-man can do it. We say "hue-man" because this is Our term for the ascended Beings you are becoming, and to make a distinction from "humans," who are still in the process. To bi-locate, you simply picture the new location firmly in your mind, then step into it. The dimensional shift occurs at the etheric/sub-aural/subconscious level, and at the cellular level. Remember when your car was almost hit by the truck that day on the road? Your Angelic Team bi-located it, and you all, to a spot a few yards further down the road so a fatal crash would not occur. In other words, you have done this before, although you did not know it! The cells dematerialize and shift to the new frequency. When you fix the new location in your mind you are subtly tuning into it, changing your frequency, altering your vibration to match that of the new location. Once your vibration ceases to resonate the "home" frequency (or channel) and begins to resonate at the "Paris" frequency, the bi-location occurs nearly instantaneously. It almost happens automatically, as the two vibrations rush to match, like magnets attracting each other. You *become* the frequency that matches the new destination, and that new destination magnetizes you there quick as a wink.

So how do you magnetize/tune/resonate/vibrate at the "Paris" frequency, rather than your own native frequency? This is a little harder, but not much. You must feel, like intention, that you are already there. You must smell, taste, see, and hear "Paris" in your Soul, and then the Universe aligns to meet your new wish. Remember Beloved, that hue-mans are co-Creators with Us in this Universe. Once you fix your will on and command something, the Universe begins to align to make it so. It is the same principle with bi-location (teleportation). Once you intend it, your vibration changes to match the new location's frequency. Once your frequency changes, the new frequency pulls you there to ensure vibrational match. In some ways it is the exact opposite of what happens when someone you were formerly close to suddenly disappears from your life – the vibrational energies between the two of you are no longer a matching pair, so the frequency shifts and "separates" you.

Let Us think of a better explanation. Go and rest, and we will wake you early.

FEBRUARY 11, 2016
AM (EARLY!), HOME

Archangel Michael:

Thank you for getting up, Beloved – We accessed your memory archives and discovered an easy way to explain how to tune your frequency and an exercise to help you practice. Remember the old Memorex poster you used to have of a man sitting in an armchair in front of a speaker, hair blowing as if in the wind? *"Is it live, or is it Memorex?"* Tuning into the new vibration/frequency/place is like this ad – you must sit quietly at first as you learn and imagine the new place. Close your eyes. Smell the Parisian croissants baking. See the Eiffel Tower off in the distance. Imagine the taste of a French pastry. Feel the gentle breeze caressing your cheek – breeze that is ventilating the room housing the Mona Lisa. *Feel it. Smell it. Taste it.* Thus, your cells know to vibrate at the "Paris" frequency, and the rest is automatic; the best explanation is two magnets slowly sliding towards each other and then snapping together. Except it is a pleasant sensation, not like magnets slamming together! There is no jolt, just a "bzzzt" as the frequency shifts. We hear the question: how

Leap and the net will
appear.
- Zen koan

do you know you won't turn up in the middle of traffic or inside a stone wall, just your fingertips hanging out? Beloved, this is not a mechanical process, like in a movie. There is no computer dialing in arbitrary coordinates. This is you, your magnificent brain and body, and your magnificent Soul. Unless you actively intend to jump into traffic or half in/half out of a tree, you simply do not. And why would you? You can always simply bi-locate yourself again in the next moment out of the tree! You will also be able to feel the vibrations and frequencies of the new place, as rocks and trees most assuredly have their own special and unique sensations as well. They are all living creatures, although some, like rocks, move and breathe so slowly you would not recognize them as such. Yes, Beloved, even rocks have their own special life force; as part of Gaia/Earth, how could they not? Water, air, soil, plants, trees, animals... each lives in harmony with its environment, living and interconnecting in this vast web we call our Universe.

We hear your other question – if you've never been to Paris, how can you imagine yourself there? At first, you may need to look at pictures of Paris or buy a croissant and eat it. But soon you will know how to sort through the vibrations available and choose. In that way, it's almost like having cable television. You have thousands of channels available at all times, but you really only watch a few, and they are marked on the remote as "presets." This would be your "home" frequency, your "default" location, and the strongest frequency. Always you can feel the strongest pull, which would be your home base, your "return to sender" location, the place where you get your mail! (laughter) To bi-locate, simply change the channel. Remember in your movie *Contact* how the lead character was listening to the stars? And how, in the space between 300.1 and 300.101 there was a definite change in sound? Such it is with the frequency shifts. Even a tiny change, hundredths or thousandths of a degree, can mean the difference between static and a clear channel, much like an old-fashioned radio with a dial.

So again, for new places, you must find the correct channel, using your intent, using your Wayfinder's Imagination (*Finding Your North Star,* by Martha Beck), and simply *go.*

FEBRUARY 12, 2016
4 AM, Home

Archangel Michael:

Thank you for arising early, Beloved! There is so much more to say, We hardly know where to begin. For now, let Us concentrate on a single topic – the human body as it was intended to be.

The thirteen strands of DNA, when connected and activated, turn on in a very specific sequence, and as the pairs "come online," more and more of the original, intended, birthright uses and abilities of the human form become possible. Yes, Beloved, use your pendulum and ask the questions if you like, or We can simply write them down here for you:

MB: Are all my thirteen DNA strands plugged in?

AAM: Yes.

MB: Are all thirteen "turned on"?

AAM: No, but they are coming online very quickly.

MB: How many are turned on?

AAM: Six (three pairs), with another two (one pair) due to come online at your next upgrade.

MB: When is that upgrade going to happen?

AAM: In March, unless you wish to postpone it [until after your big event is finished the first week of April].

MB: No, please go ahead as planned. What are the effects of this next upgrade: physical, mental, and emotional?

AAM: This is exactly what We wish to discuss today. Shall We proceed?

As originally designed by the Sirian genetics masters, the human template form was designed with thirteen strands of DNA; six pairs and a single strand that is a direct line or connection to the God-Source (also called the Universe, or the Creator). When the Draconians altered the human DNA to create a worker species, humans actually devolved into a new sub-species, genetically distinct from the original humans (the source material). This sub-species had only two connected DNA strands. We wish to say here that this is not judgmental, Beloved, nor are We saying that the new species was in any way "less" than the original; "sub" in this case refers only to two DNA strands vs. thirteen strands. In effect, the Draconians "unplugged" eleven of the strands, leaving only those which held the basest, most fundamental information: how to breathe, eat, avoid death (fear consciousness and instinct), and how to reproduce. The Draconians reasoned that this "stripped down" version of humans would be docile and subservient, perfect workers for gold mining and other manual labor.

What they did not anticipate – again, because they are stunted emotionally – was that without the other DNA strands and the thirteenth strand to bind the other strands and connect to Source, these new humans would lack the compassion necessary to achieve true survival. The humans, trapped in a seemingly dualistic world in which all but the most primitive instincts had been suppressed, killed one another in large numbers over land, food and water supplies, mating rights and rituals, perceived differences, etc. The Draconians had lost so many workers in the "downgrade," and now those who remained were killing each other off. In an attempt to correct this imbalance, the Draconians again altered the human DNA. They mutated a gene, causing testosterone levels to skyrocket, which had a dual effect – it made the male workers stronger, and brought all the females into a kind of "heat." But unlike animals, where the heat cycle only occurs once or twice a year to allow the females time to carry and bear a baby, the human heat cycle was accelerated until it reached a near-monthly cycle. This meant more females could become pregnant all through the year, thus creating more workers, more quickly. Eventually, these humans bred themselves out of any sustainable population and became like locusts, consuming every natural resource, after which they simply moved to a new area and repeated the process.

You must understand, Beloved, these humans were not evil, not purposely trying to ruin the Earth. They were simply doing what they had been designed to do: to work, to eat, and to breed. Their days were filled with mental and emotional confusion, manual labor, constant fighting over resources, and ceaseless fear of death, from starvation, childbirth, attack, exhaustion.

It was this "state of affairs" that prompted Gaia (Earth) to cry out for heavenly assistance, and help was granted as a free will request by that sentient Being. The Sirians stepped back in and implanted a virus among the population; this virus mutated the DNA yet again, causing it to unfold and a carrier gene to activate which would lead to DNA reconnection. But the process had to evolve naturally, with each successive generation having a slightly higher percentage of people carrying the "DNA Reconnection" gene. After about 52,000 years (just two cycles of the precession of the equinoxes – short in galactic time!), critical mass was achieved and the DNA reconnection gene was now present in enough individuals that the gene spontaneously switched to the "on" position. From there, things began to move very quickly; exponentially faster, in fact! Critical mass was achieved around 1948 C.E., around the same time as the Philadelphia Experiment, the end of World War II, the golden age of mass communication by radio, and television just around the corner.

We now wish to give some examples and signs, that you can begin to recognize how many DNA strands are plugged in – always remembering that each human being is unique:

2 DNA strands (one pair) plugged in: lowest chakras active (base, sacral; limited access to solar plexus); survive, find food, reproduce; emotional body intact but limited; duality and fear consciousness. Mental/emotional age = infancy. 95.6 percent of population.

4 DNA strands (two pairs) plugged in: solar plexus chakra fully activated; heart chakra open but limited; intellectual capacity at "full," beginnings of high heart communication; philosophy, higher order, and esoteric thinking; compassion active; beginnings of the

extrasensory powers (ESPs, or "clairs"). Mental/emotional age = child. 4 percent of population.

6 DNA strands (three pairs) plugged in: heart and high heart chakras fully engaged; pineal gland awakened but not yet fully receiving messages; extrasensory powers fully engaged; beginnings of physical change manifestations (body changes, other physical changes); ability to manifest in 3D/4D space in "real time;" intellectual understanding of Time, Truth, Compassion. This stage can last a long time, as it is the adolescence and young adulthood of the Soul. .01 percent of population.

8 DNA strands (four pairs) plugged in: high heart, pineal gland fully open and actively receiving; all lower chakras fully integrated; instantaneous physical manifestation of desired outcome (physical, mental, and emotional body changes); instant physical manifestation of desired objects; bi-location to any point on Earth; complete understanding and practice of self-love and compassion; all extrasensory powers fully functional and considered ordinary; soul mate retrieval, Twin Flame retrieval. Mental/emotional/physical age = thirties. .001 percent of population.

10 DNA strands (five pairs) plugged in: all chakras on and functioning optimally; unity consciousness; bi-location possible to anywhere in the known Universe. Mental/physical age = 30-35 (hold at this physical age). .0001 percent of population.

13 DNA strands (six pairs + one) plugged in: fully integrated Galactic human (Homo galacticus), able to take part in galactic meetings as a representative of Earth/Gaia consciousness; travel to all aspects of known Universe; incarnate if desired; ascension within the physical body. Fully actualized Hue-man. Until "Now," Beloved, there were only ever one or two of these Beings on Earth at any given time (Jesus, Babaji, Quan Yin, Buddha, others).

We also wish to give you some Reconnection "symptoms." Although the reconnection of DNA strands is a natural process and therefore has no disease symptoms, humans need signposts to help them recognize that they are on the right track. Signs and symptoms of upgrades, DNA reconnection, and DNA "coming online" include headaches (especially sinus headaches as the pineal gland activates); general tiredness and lethargy and an intense desire to sleep (or hyper-awakeness); allergy or flu-like symptoms; stomach upsets, as the foods one used to eat can no longer be tolerated; skin problems (release of toxins); muscle aches and pains (again, release of toxins); dizziness and nausea; irritability; erratic moods and mood swings, as the emotional body attempts to "come online" and find balance; disorientation and memory loss; and death.

Yes, Beloved, We said "death," which is another whole topic We wish to discuss, but for the purposes of this explanation, let Us simply say that some Souls' contracts do not include physical ascension with this planet. These beloved Souls agreed to end their physical lives in order to collectively strengthen the protective grid around Gaia – a task accomplished much more easily outside the physical body. All the Souls you've heard about in the news lately agreed to add their vast spiritual knowledge to the safety net surrounding Earth. Each Soul that selflessly agrees to do this task reinforces the Earth's ability to heal itself and facilitates a smoother transition for the Souls that come after.

Then there are Souls like you, Beloved, who chose a much harder task: to stay on Earth and help people Awaken out of the 3D prison of two-strand DNA. We say "harder" because, while no task is better or worse, nor more or less valued, some tasks and life missions are widely held to be so critical that they are entrusted only to the very most elite members, beings who are so beloved and trusted as to place the most precious lives of Earth's inhabitants in their hands.

You are such a One, Beloved. Our "A" Team! There are many of you, each using his or her own unique gifts to accomplish a single goal: Awakening on a mass scale. It is consciousness that triggers the DNA to re-engage, and the DNA reinserting causes a rise in consciousness, a cycle that continues up in a spiral until fully actualized hue-mans emerge, to become engaged members of the Galactic community.

We feel you are overwhelmed, Beloved – happy, scared, sad, disbelieving, proud, angry – all in seemingly equal measure. But believe Us – when you chose to accept this mission, you fully understood what would be required, and with free will, you volunteered to return to Earth a final time to help the last ascension process. This is why you were born a Leo and a leader, a communicator, a natural networker, a collaborator, and a mediator; so you could write Our Messages, bring them to the world infused with Light, and co-Create and help facilitate a mass Awakening. Did you see how quickly you picked your pen back up? You are eager to fulfill your mission – and you have more help than you can imagine!

Your next upgrade was scheduled for March, but after your profound realization today, We can do it sooner. It is your free will choice. Do you wish to accelerate now?

Michele:

[Crying at the magnitude of this Message] *Yes!*

Archangel Michael:

Go and rest. Thy will be done.

FEBRUARY 14, 2016
AM, Home

Archangel Michael:

Suddenly, Beloved, "Happy Valentine's Day" means something more than the card and chocolates holiday... It is a day to celebrate all the people you love – how wonderful that your mind and your worldview expand so quickly!

You do not see the extent of the changes because you are inside them, but if you could see – and your ability to see grows and improves daily – you would see someone who is much different than the person you were at Christmas, and even different from the person you were last week. Yes, Beloved, We know that linear time terms don't really apply, but they remain a convenient way to explain the changes that are occurring! Yes, We will give you some examples. Your eyesight has indeed improved – almost instantly after the upgrade your vision had returned to the level it was about four years ago. It will jump again here very soon and return to your early-thirties level of perfect vision. You have also noticed that your skin has improved slightly and attributed it to the medicine. The medicine was but the external signal – like the red pill that allowed Morpheus to track Neo [in the movie The Matrix]. In truth, your DNA was already shifting to accommodate the changes from the upgrade to eight strands. You see, because nothing is linear, changes could begin to occur even before the so-called initiating act – in this case, the upgrade you received yesterday. Thank you for going straight in to lie down and sleep; it is so much easier to perform the upgrade when you command it and set aside specific time for it.

The irritation you experienced with your friend was a reflection of her state of mind – you were mirroring her back to herself, although at that moment, neither of you was doing it consciously. This will also be your work – consciously being a mirror for people so they can see their own behavior and change it if they choose. You will also have the mission to raise the vibration of such encounters; instead of merely mirroring, you will model transformation from irritation to contentment, for example. This is their chance to see someone (you!) move from the state they're in, to contentment, and know that it's possible. In some cases, just this knowledge is enough to spur change.

You are already good at mirroring – you are an NF [Intuitive, Feeling from the Meyers-Briggs Personality Inventory] who learned to be an ST [Sensing, Thinking]! You will do this daily without even knowing you are doing it. You are indeed receiving Our communication image clearly – of you raising the vibrations of hundreds of people at a book signing, and later, of thousands of people at your speeches.

"...sometimes I've believed
as many as six impossible
things before breakfast."
- Lewis Carroll
(Alice in Wonderland)

This is a gift – part of the "suite" of gifts related to your mission of Awakening. And yes, Beloved, the Spa is part of it, too. You always intuitively felt that if people were surrounded by beautiful water, trees, sunshine – and if they were cared for and pampered – it would literally change them. And you are right! The Spa is still in your future, if you choose that path when the time comes.

Regarding Wayne: Beloved, We feel your distress at the thought that We lied to you, or that possibly you are not receiving Our Messages correctly. Neither is correct. When we implanted the mission for you to reconnect with Wayne, We did so with a goal in mind – for you to remind him of his worth as a human being, and to begin the task of Awakening him. We thought you would eventually meet in person. His responsibilities at work, with his parents, and at home have drained this vital aspect – his humanity – his right to be appreciated as a person (and not as purely a father, for example). This part is out of balance, and you have been placed in his path to be a breathing reminder of his worth as a person and as a man (in a similar capacity as Edward once reminded you of your worth as a woman). We still feel your distress at having moved the pendulum yourself rather than allowing the pendulum to be moved by Us. We did not correct you then because it made no difference to your mission, which is about *Wayne*. Fear not, Beloved. We always protect you and guide you. When you listen quietly, you always hear Us. And in the very rare cases where you "get it wrong," We will notify you, as we did this time. We feel you dwelling on "what-if" and "what-would-have-been," but your Soul contract did not include a marriage to Wayne, and the security and family that would have resulted. This is too small a life for you, Beloved. Once again, We wish to assure you these are not judgments, but rather for your own journey, you could not have such attachments. Now, all children are your children, and all humans are your lovers. And you have experienced loss, which will allow you to identify and understand this, your mission.

We feel your human hunger calling – go and eat, and we shall speak again.

FEBRUARY 15, 2016
PM, Home

Archangel Michael:

Your irritation, Beloved, is part hormonal, part fatigue, and part mission. Your friend brings drama and irritation to the table, so you must reflect it back to her. What you must do is reflect, and then uplift; this is the true purpose of this mission – to make a better condition on Earth. Also, you must learn when the drama is yours, and when it is you reflecting someone else's. There is a very distinct energy signature or imprint, and you will not wonder again once you have the two energies clearly defined in your mind.

You have been watching [the 1999 TV series] Roswell, and We have impulsed you to watch it, because the "alien powers" from the show are very much like the "powers" humans have when the DNA is plugged in. The aliens can change molecular structure, "read minds," heal injuries, attract or repulse physical objects, and create a barrier to keep things out (although yours is not green!). (laughter) The character who can "mind warp" is a stretch of an actual ability, although by the time anyone reached a stage where having this ability was imminent, she or he would never use it to force another person's free will. By the time a being has that many DNA strands plugged in and functioning, the sense of "right" and "wrong" is pretty advanced (even taking into account that the concepts do not even exist!).

Your mission as you experience it now is one of slight apprehension and frustration, but this is as it should be – these are early days yet. Also the eight-strand upgrade you received earlier is "knocking your system for a loop" as they say – you feel almost manic to Us, Beloved, as your energy is vibrating so fast. It also explains how you were able to clean your house so quickly, when it would have taken you so much longer in a previous time. Even your writing speed has increased, and We have increased your manual dexterity to compensate. Soon it will be time to type these Messages, and you will have a break for your handwriting, although not for your hands! (laughter)

These DNA upgrades have been the fodder for so many Messages because this is consuming the bulk of your brain's capacity at the moment. Your system is working at what is essentially three-times-speed, and the physical manifestations are already beginning to show. You have lost some weight, your eyesight has improved, and your sugar craving has diminished as well. Your skin continues to improve, and some is mechanical (when it itches, you scratch it, which causes irritation, and more scratching). We will implant a no-scratching rule! (laughter) No, really!

Begin to pull together your resource and other materials – you have a good start but there will be more coming. Rest now and call your mother. You need a break!

FEBRUARY 16, 2016
PM, Home

Archangel Michael:

We wish to speak tonight of the Spa – still a destiny for you, and one more step in your mission of Awakening humanity. You have long wondered, Beloved, if it was true that people behaved and felt differently in beautiful surroundings, and yes, they do. When a person is at leisure to enjoy himself and to simply relax, a marvelous change occurs, and the cells begin to regenerate. Tensions ease, stress decreases, and people simply *are*. The Spa will be such a place, and [people] will Awaken there. We have a certain kind of water We wish you to have in the pools – the copper-infused form that Mr. Anderson told you about. Long have humans known of the healing power of water, and of the healing power of mineralized hot springs. Copper is one such element that provides many benefits, and as Mr. Anderson pointed out, it feels like swimming in silk. It is good for the skin, and for the bones and ligaments as well. People will come to the Spa seeking relaxation and amusement, but they will get so much more! So, Beloved, the Spa is still coming.

Sleep now, and We will ease your dreams. There is a minor adjustment to the new upgrade systems, and We will do this. You will awaken refreshed and rested. Good night!

FEBRUARY 17, 2016
AM, Home

Archangel Michael:

Beloved, the reason you woke up confused and tired is *sugar*. It's the same process as drinking too much – you wake up logy and exhausted. We have removed the urge for sugar – now the change must be fully integrated, and you must *cooperate*. There are no habits anymore! You did indeed receive an adjustment last night, and that also contributed to your poor sleep. We urge you again to go to bed earlier and get up earlier – you will feel so much better – you know this. We understand you enjoy being awake at night, and you can, but the result is poorer sleep and a hard start the next day. Use your free will to decide which you prefer.

Our topic today is what you call the "time warp." As you know, "time" (little "t") does not exist, and thus it is flexible and bendable. You are capable of warping time; every hue-man is. You know from experience that happy moments seem fleeting, while sad ones seem to last forever. This is an example every person understands. Children are Masters of Time; they live perpetually in the moment and are happy because of it. This concept bears more discussion. Let's talk again tonight.

(LATER THAT SAME DAY)

A "time warp" occurs when the Ego's awareness of a linear timescape temporarily fragments and the Ego's sense of time/space merges with the All That Is. In other words, when the Ego forgets to be vigilant about perceiving time (little "t") – which is just an accident of the way your five senses process the electronic and magnetic information – then a "time warp" occurs. In reality, the "time warp" is an example of *true* Time (capital "T"), which is amusing, considering most humans consider linear time to be "real" and the perceived time warp to be the temporary illusion, when in fact the reverse is true! So, Beloved, when you said that your regularly warped time, you were in fact understanding that you are spending more and more time in the glorious Now! These Messages, incidentally, are written entirely in the Now, and We know to "wrap it up" and stop when your linear mind re-engages. You don't hear Us nearly so well when you are in time (small "t").

So, how to create a "time warp" – how to be in the Now? There are many ways, but the way We choose to share here is to remember to breathe and observe. Try not to analyze, or judge, but simply observe. Feel how lovely the sun feels on your feet, how nice the weather is. Listen to the birds twittering on the feeder, and the patter of birdseed as it is flung down from the feeder. Smell the fresh air! Every "moment" contains an Eternity, is special, and perfect, and glorious. This is the realization – that every single moment is another Now, and you can enjoy it exactly as-is. As your Matt Kahn says, "Whatever arises, love that." This is so wise, and this beloved hue-man is a very clear channel for Our Messages. He is absolutely in his mission 100 percent of the "time"! (laughter) You, We are proud of you as well. You feel your mission stronger and stronger each day.

We applaud you for making the free will choice to accept your divine gift of writing and the time you've dedicated to this so far. We know you feel bad sometimes when you need to stop – because your hand hurts, or you're tired, or your attention wanders – but never are We cross or unhappy with you! Always, We feel happy and proud that you choose over and over again to hear Us and record these Messages. We feel your excitement as the pages add up and as you realize that two notebooks will simply not contain everything We wish to share! We are never disappointed in you – here, there is no judgment on an individual's free will choice. We do, however, rejoice gladly when We see our "Earth Angels" accept their tasks and missions wholeheartedly and make them a constant life choice to be enjoyed and savored. And We feel that writing for you is not a burden, and that when circumstances prevent you from writing as much or as often as you'd like, you feel guilty and disappointed. You don't need guilt or disappointment – only perseverance – all is coming along well! Fear not, the book is coming, and we are still "on schedule," if such a thing really exists! (laughter). All is in divine right timing with the book, and the potentials solidify further each day and with each page you transcribe – for that is what you are doing, Beloved: listening and transcribing.

Enough of time warps – next We wish to speak with you about health, and the free-will choices each person makes regarding his health, or lack of health. First,

We wish to remind you that "health" is a free will choice, as is each other element of your Earthly life. While some illnesses are borne of contracts formed and chosen in the Interlife, most illness is the result of old programming interfering with your current reality. Take the example of a heart attack. A person may be so sad, he may literally choose a "heart break" in the form of a physical manifestation. Cancer may be the result of feeling so abandoned and rejected that one's own body literally rejects its fellow cells. Many of these issues, although not all, are the result of leftover unprocessed, suppressed feelings and thoughts and emotions from previous incarnations on Earth. Take the example of the three death scenes you witnessed during your last past life regression session – being drowned, falling and hitting your head, and as a fish being bitten in half by a shark. In each case, your incarnate body died from head trauma, and in the present incarnation you experience headaches, exactly along the "fault lines" of the water, the head injury, and the bite line. You have other repressed emotions as well, but with the work you have previously done and with your recent upgrade to eight strands of DNA, We can tell you that much of this additional work was "comped," divinely commuted to allow faster completion of your assigned mission.

I am not sure if you fully realize, Beloved, but when you cried a few days ago during one of our Transmissions, you fully and completely accepted – with free will intact, and divinely inspired and ordained – that your mission to write this book was cemented here on the 4D physical plane. We had anticipated it would take a few more weeks of writing before you fully integrated and accepted this, which is why your upgrade was scheduled for March. But this was the signpost We had been waiting for, and you surprised Us with your willingness and eagerness to get going! Free will is indeed a beautiful law, Beloved! So, after acceptance of your mission and after that afternoon's upgrade, the decision was made between you and your Team (yes, you were here and part of the discussion!) to "check off" much of the clearing work you had left to do (although there was, relatively speaking, not that much left, something akin to allowing an advanced eleventh grader to graduate early). Yes, you have done that much internal work! Also, you should know that writing these Messages has changed you indelibly and has accelerated the eight strand DNA processing. The more you write, the "righter" you become! (laughter) We feel your hand cramping, so We will finish the health discussion soon. Thank you, Beloved, for your service!

FEBRUARY 18, 2016
PM, Home

Archangel Michael:

Good evening, Beloved, and welcome to the new Now! your enjoyable evening out with friends and family is an example of how interactions are in 5D – all parties enjoying the company of the collective and contributing equally to the enjoyment of the event. Look forward to many more of these!

Tonight, We wish to speak about money in the new age. There is already plenty for everyone, but because many people still live most of their lives in fear consciousness, scarcity appears to be real. The exact opposite is actually True, Beloved! There is plenty of everything for every human on the planet, and for every need to be met in a way that is sustainable, ecologically and environmentally responsible, and with great care for the humans receiving it. The Universe is a vast place, Beloved, and it is full of wonders – *there is enough!* The issues your race faces now are the direct result of misuse by a few dark souls who seek to enslave humans and keep them subservient. For when a person is consumed by the fear that he cannot feed himself and his family, and worried about whether or not he can pay the rent, he is kept in a low vibration/frequency, a state that keeps his mind clogged up with unnecessary chatter and distress. Only when humans Awaken can they see these systems (finances, education, religion, politics, health care, etc.) as they truly are – prisons for your mind and your Soul.

Chief among these prisons is the misused tool you call money. Currency is just pieces of paper; coins are just bits of metal – they have no intrinsic value in and of themselves, but they are locked away in bank vaults, and guarded by alarms and men with weapons. All this is an illusion; those bits of colored paper are no more real – and no more valuable – than the numbers on the computer screen. At least if the servers all crashed, you'd still have the actual pieces of paper and circles of metal! But the real mistake comes in the human's reactions and perceptions of money. Money is simply frozen energy, temporarily coalesced into a slip of paper with numbers and pictures on it, just as a book is frozen energy, or a chair, or a spoon, or a pocket watch. Money's only value lies in its perceived ability to manifest desired items. You trade your little pieces of paper (or slide your rectangle of plastic through a slot) for an orange or a bicycle. When humans realize how easy it is to manifest desired items – clothing, books, food, furniture... anything! – there will be no need for money. But before most humans reach this stage of DNA insertion and are able to instantly manifest, there will be a financial revolution. Funds will be available to all, and every human will enjoy the benefits of living well according to his or her own tastes and needs.

What prompted the creation of money in the first place? At one time, each person simply contributed to the welfare of the whole. Farmers shared their crops among all villagers, mothers looked after all the village children, and the hunters shared the meat with everyone. At some point, someone decided to keep and use more than his fair share. For example, the hunter rationalized that since he had done the work to hunt the animal, he should benefit solely from the kill. The farmers followed suit, saying they had worked the fields alone – why should they share?

Perhaps next a village woman offered to trade some beads for a bowl of corn, and the farmer agreed, thinking his wife would have the most beautiful necklace in the village. But when the woman ran out of beads, she asked for more corn, and perhaps the farmer gave it to her, perhaps on "credit." Eventually everyone was hungry, or thirsty, or had no childcare help because everyone owed everyone else. Perhaps they began keeping track of these "owed debts" by exchanging small bits of metal. Well, you can see where all this went. The village woman with "nothing to trade" soon became an outcast and "lesser-than" because she owed so many people, and the farmer's wife with her fancy beads became "more-than" because she didn't have to work.

But We see the potentials aligning for a great shift in this area very soon, Beloved. You will see this in the next five to ten years, a complete overhaul of a system that as it is now, serves nobody except the top one percent of the top one percent.

FEBRUARY 20, 2016
AM, Home

Archangel Michael:

Good morning, Beloved! Your visit to Lelon yesterday gave you much to ponder and consider. Yes, Beloved; your relationship to him is becoming that of a spiritual mentor and the friendship is built on mutual respect – this is good!

As ever, he was correct about many things: your continuing quest to stand in your own power, and strongly, and to temper that with the need to remain humble. Such is the "danger" for Leos, Beloved – you sometimes forget it is *through* you, and not *from* you. Your Matt Kahn is very good at remembering this, and when you speak to him, he can tell you how he does it. In your case, your mother will serve as a grounding person, to remind you of this fact and to ensure your head doesn't get too big!

We feel your distress at not writing yesterday, and you thought about it so many times. This is how free will works, Beloved. You can pursue any path you choose, from moment to moment. As it happens, We are delighted that you chose to take a break and take a nap. There were a few upgrades We needed to tweak, and that gave us time to do them. The physical changes continue – your outer shell is regressing to that of a thirty-five-year-old, and your internal organs are becoming those of a twenty-year-old, new and healthy. As We have said before, you do not notice it because you are in it, but someone who had not seen you in months would immediately sense a change. We can sense your impatience so let us begin today with a discussion of Love, and how it differs from love (small "l"). We have waited until now to bring up this important topic because it touches you so near your heart, and you are now ready – since the upgrade to eight strands of DNA – to learn the Truth.

Love (capital "L") is another absolute construct, like Time (capital "T") and Compassion (capital "C"). In fact, "Compassion" and "Love" are very nearly interchangeable, except that "Compassion" is a state of mind and a way of life, and "Love" is really a verb. It is sad that the word "love" has been used so frequently on your Earth, but that was done deliberately to dilute its meaning. When commercials urge you to love your clean-smelling laundry and to love your new lipstick, the real meaning is lost. On the one hand, a person who is Awake may be so happy and in tune with herself that she may indeed experience bliss from the simple sensory experience of smelling fresh laundry, or admire and love herself especially well when she feels beautiful (thanks to the new lipstick). But overall, the trend to use the word "love" in these contexts simply muddies the waters.

Love (capital "L") is a force of the Universe – a guiding principle of All That Is. We feel your confusion, Beloved, and We wish to phrase all this differently now. We have adapted and changed Our minds; We exercised the prerogative of our feminine aspects! (laughter) Perhaps the dark, the lower vibrational forces, intended to dilute the word "love" by applying it indiscriminately to lipstick and laundry detergent, but as ever, the Grand Design proved the winner. We rejoice at so many people "loving" their laundry, or "loving" their new lipstick and feeling more beautiful – as a whole concept, more "love," no matter what the form, is a good thing!

"Love" (capital "L") is another name for "Light," and is the very fabric, the very stuff of life and creation. Love (capital "L") is how the Universe was made, and ties into sacred geometry in a very specific way. (See appendix D)

In the Beginning, Creator decided to play a game – Creator wanted to experience All There Is, so Creator split into seven Universes, and in each Universe It placed a God, a being whose task it was to run the game and oversee the rules. In this Universe, the game is "free will." Other Universes have different rules, but in this one, each Being is allowed to make any choice, or no choice. God, who was really an equal slice of Creator, created space, and planets, and stars, and microbes, and then let the experiment run itself, only imposing rules to keep the game going...

We feel your attention wandering, Beloved. Shall We talk again later?

There is no equal
to you.
- Bhagavad Gita

FEBRUARY 21, 2016
AM, HOME

Archangel Michael:

The last few days have been frustrating for you, Beloved. You are wondering if all this is real, if you are hearing Us correctly, and if the interview you read from a 1947 alien is true. We will happily speak with you about all these things.

First, Beloved, Ascension is most certainly real, and you and the planet are indeed experiencing it, as are all the other beings on this planet – indeed, all planets in your solar system. Each person, as a unique expression of Divine Creation, is doing so in a unique way, but since all things are fractally connected and since All There Is encompasses everything, you are all doing this process as a group; indeed, since you are connected to Us, there is overflow, or overlap "here" as well. Remember, your game, your mission, was to use your free will to experience everything possible and to add to the Akashic Records, the Universal Encyclopedia, each experience having its own detailed entry, its own section, within the Akash. This, humans have admirably done, and the collective wisdom has grown so much that the entire planet is able to Ascend together. Gone are the possibilities that once said that only 144,000 would make it while the rest perished. Remember, Beloved, every being "ascends" when he or she "dies," so this is something very ordinary.

The difference this time is that you are readying to Ascend within the body and with all memories intact. "To date," only a very, very few humans have managed this, among them your Buddha, your Babaji, your Jesus, and a few others. In fact, Beloved, all these beings were in reality a single being returning multiple times in multiple bodies (tailored to match the needs and expectations of that time and place), but the Oversoul of each remained the same. This enlightened being is a great servant of humanity and has incarnated many times to assist other humans at key points along the Ascension timeline. (Yes, Beloved, there is no such thing as "time" but remember, Time does exist in the sense that events and experiences occur in their own Divine Right Timing.)

So yes, Beloved, Gaia/Earth and all her inhabitants are indeed Ascending. You yourself have experienced these symptoms, and mistaken them for ordinary headaches, stomachaches, tiredness, etc. But more often than not, these physical effects are caused by physical shifts in energy pattern assimilation by your incarnate form. They have been relatively slight in you over your lifetime, Beloved; yes, We feel that you think this is incredible – you are remembering mumps, mono, chicken pox, headaches, toothaches. But We also see others who suffer daily, Beloved, from heart and liver failure, cancer, poisoning, and more. When compared to your beloved aunt's constant health challenges, for example, your own health history has been uneventful and benign. These are the things you must remember, and the things for which gratitude will help the most. *Knowing* your health is good, *knowing* you hear us clearly, *knowing* you are being taken care of – all this coalesces with each expression of gratitude, and the Universe bends to conform to your commands.

We feel your distress at the interview you read. Yes, Beloved, the Being who spoke the interview was from another planet, but then most lifeforms on Earth originated on other planets! He was a "Grey," and as such his emotional body is somewhat less developed than an ordinary human's. Everything he said was his truth (small "t"), from his point of view. To someone actively blocking Ascension due to fear, Earth would indeed feel like a prison planet. It does have relatively high gravity, its land masses do indeed float over a molten layer (but not the core), and there are indeed volcanoes and tidal waves. The last pole shift did indeed create an increase in the sea level, wiping out virtually all land-based lifeforms (yes, that did occur). And yes, the 3D duality consciousness is indeed a "trap," as it brings with it amnesia and a perceived disconnection from the God-Source. Some of this was by design, Beloved! To experience everything possible within the context of free will (remember, that's our "game" in this Universe: free will), some experiences will appear "negative" or "bad." But in reality, all energy just *is*. All experiences just *are*. There is no good, no bad, no high, no low. Just Divine Balance and the absolute free will to experience anything you can dream of! So yes, to someone looking at Earth from a perspective of depravity, insanity, and lack, this is what that being will experience. Remember, the Universe is simply a big magnet. Whatever frequency you tune to, the Universe magnetizes the corresponding thoughts, behaviors, actions, and items to you. If you don't like the way it's going, choose again! Your free will is in charge of your experiences 110% of the time. Each human absolutely, unerringly creates his own reality all the time, right down to the weather! This is enough for now Beloved. Please, let's speak again later today.

(LATER THAT SAME DAY)
PM, HOME

Your symptoms are decreasing, and tonight We will upgrade you again so that the changes will implement even faster. Already you have assimilated the faster frequency and your writing is faster and smoother. Soon you will begin writing in the morning and at night as the book moves into the next phase. We feel your hesitation and we assure you that all is well and there will be plenty of time for all. We know how important it is for you not to disappoint, and you will not.

Your father is part of this, too, although he does not know it yet, and he tends to look first inside the comforts of his scientific model. Nevertheless, he will see and comprehend the truth of the scientific and metaphysical words We write. He will be proud of your success, Beloved, and if the potentials continue, his "shell" will crack open and let even more Light in. This book will help him, even if he never reads it, because he is part of your journey and you have been beaming light to him for some time. Just think how much has changed since you saw him last summer! You have discovered your mission so clearly and have begun living the life you came here to live. This is happening! All your "dreams" – which were really implanted memories from your session in the Interlife – are coming true; you set it up that way! And your happiness is present, Beloved. We heard you today loving yourself, and the weather, and your house. This is the fastest way to get more of what you want, Beloved. Gratitude! You know this! What a blessing that your mission should be to share these amazing words with others!

Another section coming tomorrow early, so expect Us to wake you.

FEBRUARY 22, 2016
AM, HOME

Archangel Michael:

We gently remind you to ask to speak only to Us, and to ask that Messages only from Us are received. Lelon has told you this, and it is true – that you are a spiritual warrior for the Light, and that your "weapon" is the pen. Your book, infused as it is with Love-Light, will Awaken all who read it, or even touch the cover. Unfortunately, all the examples for things spreading wildly are negative: wildfire, infectious disease, cancer. We will think of a positive example and this is the book. Even the workers who package it at the factory will feel the effects! And each person becomes a "carrier" as well, spreading the Awakening in ever-widening circles. This is a glorious destiny, Beloved, and one We know you'll really enjoy. All you have to do is be yourself! Write what you hear, follow your instincts (our impulsed messages to you), and We will guide the process.

You are wondering, Beloved, if you are the only one – if you are alone. No; there are many times many working to spread our celestial message, and many whose missions are similar to yours. It would be fair to say that you know many of these Souls' names already: Ken Carey, Drunvalo Melchizedek, Kathleen McGowan, Martha Beck, Matt Kahn, and many others. Although each writer has his or her own unique way of telling the tale, each is committed to putting more Truth into the Universe. The special thing about this particular "time" is that critical mass has been achieved, the tipping point has come... the spiral has entered the point! This information is seeping through the cracks of every country and every Mind, and those whose missions dictate that they sing it, or write it, or draw it, have been Awakened! We here in the Celestial Realms are overjoyed to see the Light pouring into Gaia. All will be well. All manner of things is already well!

Today we wish to speak to you of death and rebirth, a cycle that exists no longer. Around 1948, this cycle ended; critical mass had been achieved and there was no longer any need for humans to continue to collect data – they could concentrate on clearing out the remaining "residue" and living well. There were still problems on Earth – at least what appeared to be problems – and humans believed nothing had changed. So long had they lived in chaos and fear, that they couldn't see freedom just at the ends of their noses.

In the old system, people's bodies "wore out" and "got sick" and eventually they "died," whereupon their shells began to break down. This is logical, but incorrect. The human body is a magnificent biological machine: it is self-healing, self-replicating, self-cleansing, and when cared for at a minimum capacity, designed to last many hundreds of years. It is a shame that so many humans accept the premise that they will die at seventy, or eighty, or even ninety years of age, when your machine is designed for over 300 years of use!

So, what happened – what changed – to cause the machines to "break" so quickly? There were several factors. First and foremost, humans believe their bodies will only last eighty years. Thus do they resonate with the frequency of a short lifespan, and the Universe magnetizes that experience into their realms of existence. This frequency explanation is the first and most correct "reason," but there are others, too. The fewer pairs of DNA that are plugged in, the shorter the lifespan. A being with only two strands of DNA on and functioning cannot hope to achieve longevity – the codes simply do not exist. As critical mass was achieved with the DNA reconnection gene, every human's DNA sequence was switched on in the late 1940s (Vessel's parents' time of birth). Every single human now on Earth has all DNA reconnected (re-plugged in) – this happened spontaneously when the switch flipped "on." Now begins the process of turning on the various pairs, until everyone on Earth has all twelve strands and one master strand "turned on," the thirteenth strand being the master strand and the divine connection to Source.

As usual with other processes of this kind, the first layers take longest, and once you reach eight strands (four pairs), things speed up dramatically. Think of a pyramid or a spiral – the lower levels would take longer to complete but ultimately provide a stable base upon which the later levels build more and more quickly.

With only two strands of DNA turned "on," the human body does not have access to enough power/energy/Light to last very long. Think of a car engine never given any oil, transmission fluid, or replacement fan belt. This a two-strand body. (By the way, scientists confirm two strands of DNA; every child knows this. They do not see the other eleven strands because they are not visible until they are "on," as they exist on a frequency that cannot be seen by the physical eyes.) But as the other DNA sequences are switched on, more things become possible. You can drive an old car for a long time if it has been well-maintained!

At the end of about eighty or ninety years, a being with only two strands of DNA turned on will be like a car that has never had an oil change or a tune up. It has been driven hard with no maintenance. The body detaches from the web/Soul connection and it disintegrates; "death" occurs. This is normal in the current 3D Earth worldview, but highly unusual for other species and sentient beings which also inhabit physical bodies. Physical bodies (We refer to them as "vehicles") can easily be repaired, upgraded, reconfigured, etc., rendering "death" unnecessary. To unplug from a vehicle and allow (expect!) the vehicle to "rust away" is inherently wasteful, although other species do possess technology not widely available on Earth. Very soon enough humans will know how to repair their own vehicles, and "death" will end.

But for now, what happens when you "die"? The etheric body and the Soul connection break from the physical vehicle, which is but a shell, or a "meat suit" which your Soul temporarily inhabits, and the body becomes inanimate. The body can be packed into storage (this is misleading – in reality, it simply reverts back to energy and the *pattern* is stored in the Akashic Records for a future time when someone might want to re-experience that physical vehicle), or another Soul may choose to "step into" the vehicle as-is. This is all part of the free will contract created among all parties in the Interlife. In such a case, the new Soul is commonly referred to as a "walk-in." Usually this switchover happens when a physical vehicle experiences a serious illness or injury – at those times it is easier for one Soul to exit and another to enter.

But if a physical vehicle is vacated, and no new Soul walks in, the physical vehicle begins to return to Source energy. All physical objects are made of atoms vibrating in close proximity and are not "solid" as such, even though it appears so to the naked eye; the atoms in the shell/vehicle/body move further apart and the body returns to dispersed Source energy. Understand, Beloved, this is common and expected on Earth, but in most other parts of the galaxy, beings don't waste their vehicles by allowing them to rot! They purposefully "de-resolve" them into storage (the Akashic Records) and then they can be reconstituted quite quickly, should the situation arise. Once a body has "died," the Soul simply re-enters All That Is (although "re-enters" is not precisely correct, as the Soul *never left in the first place*). The body disintegrates (returns to atoms/returns to Source) and the Soul chooses its next mission.

The new part about what humans are doing now is that when they Ascend (return to Source or All That Is), they will take their bodies (vehicles) with them. The etheric barrier surrounding Earth and preventing this exact occurrence is nullified by the extra DNA strands that are now turning on. Think of it like a shield around a starship; if you can match the shield's frequency, you can fly right through it; but if you can't match the frequency, you are trapped by the shield.

FEBRUARY 24, 2016
AM, HOME

Archangel Michael:

Good morning, Our Beloved Vessel! We are so proud of you and the many talents you are manifesting on Earth/Gaia at this time! We applaud your dedication to these Messages, but also to the heartfelt apology you made to Our Wayne yesterday. He was indeed very hurt when you sent him home that day. We of course do not assign blame, nor do We say there was a victim, nor a perpetrator; as you know, and as We have said many times, humans unerringly create their own reality at every turn, in every moment. Your relationship with Our Wayne was an early test, set up by you (and him) to see if you would accept less than your Divine Right of unconditional Love; and you *passed* – you did not agree to go back into a relationship where you felt you'd had to do more than your fair share (as you had so many times with Charlie). Wayne was the perfect player – he loved you but wouldn't say it; he wanted to marry you but didn't ask. All this he did, perfectly, according to your pre-birth/Interlife arrangement. He has been a better friend to you than you knew (until now!).

We are pleased to tell you that we are coming close to the end of what We wish to tell you – at least for this book – but there's lots more; don't worry! Soon we will impulse you to begin typing these Messages and arranging them in a very specific order. This book will be a daily meditation book with longer discourses on several subjects such as Time, Truth, etc. Begin collecting the quotes you love, one per day, so you will need many.

Go and work. We will speak again.

You dance inside my chest.
- Rumi

FEBRUARY 25, 2016
AM, Home

Archangel Michael:

Thank you for arising when We awakened you, Beloved – there is much more to say, and little time in which to say it. Soon the book leaves your precious hands and becomes a wondrous vehicle of Awakening and Ascension! Your mother gave you a vital piece of the puzzle when she mentioned the "spiritual industry" is worth four billion dollars per year. This is no accident! Humans are hungry for real information, anything that will help them understand the seemingly-awful changes they've been experiencing – any way out of the deep hole which they perceive themselves to be in. People want answers, and their institutions are not providing satisfactory ones. The money system as it stands now serves few. The [United States] health care system seems to rely on prescription medications and surgery, and is tremendously expensive, even with Universal Healthcare. [U.S.] education is a recitation of dry facts that have little bearing on world issues. Church, once a place of refuge for many, no longer serves as a beacon, but has been reduced to a weekly social gathering. Yes, Beloved, We feel that you are coming from a perspective of the United States of America, and a mostly-Christian, White background. But your Message will seem familiar to many, and it is a universal call going out. Planet-wide, people are stirring, and the systems designed for older times and for smaller human minds are no longer working.

Beloved, We find it amusing that now, with eight strands "on" and your antennae fully engaged, that you doubt your ability to hear Us. You are – and always have been – receiving Us quite clearly, although sometimes you are distracted by life, but this is to be expected! Only part of your mission is this book; the rest is living *well.*

We feel your attention wandering, so go and have your day. Perhaps We will impulse you to write more later.

FEBRUARY 28, 2016
Midday, Home

Archangel Michael:

We feel your distress at not having written for two days, Beloved. Believe Us, We are not angry or disappointed in you, and you shall not be, either. You needed a break to assimilate the changes inherent in the last download/upgrade (from six to eight strands of DNA), which was one reason We wondered if you would choose it so soon. This is a "leap" upgrade, similar to the one between two and four strands, and is an exhausting process if there is insufficient time to rest. The eight-strand level is one where you begin to really experience the physical manifestations, and We say to you in all seriousness that the teleportation you've longed for will soon be a reality. You will also meet your Twin Flame very soon, and there will be an instant connection there! Your plans to travel will soon pick back up as well; soon, your life will be little besides travel! You must remember how to travel well, Beloved, and not to use your own body energy, but rather to tap into the limitless Universal source that is available at all times to every soul. This is truly a perpetual energy source – plenty for everybody! We invite you to use as much as you want and need, for there is an ocean available, and even the most powerful beings use only a tiny amount. You could no more use up the Universal energy than you could empty the ocean with a teaspoon! Truly, Beloved, the whole Universe is this way – enough for all, abundance for all, and more than enough Love for every single Being to exist in perfect happiness and harmony for all time. This is a wondrous Universe, made all the more wondrous by the fact that free will exists and is honored above all… which means that beings *choose* such abundance, Beloved! They actively choose to experience Love, and devotion, and sorrow, and loss – truly, the range of what is possible is vast and many-layered; it contains many tones, flavors, and colors! This is a place of infinite beauty, limitless potential, extraordinary capacity, *and you are Alive within it*! Does this not dazzle your every sense? Invigorate your very Spirit?

We also wish to congratulate you on your successful integration of the lesson a former friend gave you – to stand in your own power and not to allow another's fears or excitement to become your own. Truly, you have learned this, or you wouldn't have been able to read the article about this woman in the newspaper without being upset. She is on a very different path than you are, and she is not yet fully Awake. Have compassion for one who feels she is nothing, and who manifests cancer to prove it. She was literally eating herself away. She is stronger now and will continue to integrate as her unique pathway unfolds.

Do you see the pattern here, Beloved? You attract to yourself people who require extraordinary love, and you give it; you have been healing since you were a little girl! This book will be another manifestation of this healing power, for it is your destiny to Awaken and heal – this is your gift and why you chose to come back to Earth during this tumultuous time – this extraordinary time! – this last time.

We love you so much – We stand ready to assist you at all moments, and We invite you to begin claiming your rewards now. There is no more, "When I'm thinner, I'll be happy." There is no more, "When I'm rich, I'll be worthy." No! The time is Now. Embrace your gifts, your rewards, your challenges, and then *let go.* We will catch you.

MARCH 2, 2016
PM, HOME

Archangel Michael:

See, Beloved, We upgraded your DNA and you are already manifesting! All is in perfect, divine order – you are doing so well, We rejoice with you in the Celestial Realms as on Earth. Truly, these synchronicities are the usual state of being and quite ordinary – We applaud you for feeling and recognizing them.

Now that you are truly, fully Awake, the real fun can begin – exploring places you never could have gone, eating foods you never could have guessed, these are all coming up very soon. These will manifest and more. Did you notice the physical changes yet? Weight loss? Improved skin tone? Better vision? Less allergies? Yes, this is real – you didn't imagine any of it. and yes, your man arrives soon, too. We would tell you his name: Don (David? Doug? We tell you now: his name is not "Bubba.") (laughter). No last name for now! "D" in numerology is four, and four is the number of stability; you know this! But Don is Awake and ready to meet you, and this time, there will be no need to change. You will be equal and complete, each to himself and herself, so no compromising yourself or changing to please the other. Truly, "a match made in Heaven!"

Regarding your jobs, you will finish out your term through June, and then We have other work for you to do, other missions. And yes, you heard that right; they involve photography. Wonderful times lie around the next corner – We love you so much, Beloved. This is here to stay, so enjoy it and stop worrying that the shoe will drop.

Good night –

MARCH 3, 2016
PM, HOME

Archangel Michael:

Hello again, Beloved – it was a joy for us to see your reaction to Beth's wedding news. You were genuinely happy for her, which can only be a reaction of a person who is content and happy. The book draws to a close now. You will begin typing our words and rearranging and editing. Again, We will guide you and you will do much in a very short amount of time. Soon, the book will be a physical reality. We will take care of the publisher; your grandmother is helping! We love her purple energy, and the butterflies she loved: symbols of transformation and beauty. This is how you must be, Beloved; an embodiment of beauty and transformation. We love you so much! We will speak again, and the synchronicities will be daily from now on!

MARCH 5, 2016
PM, HOME

Archangel Michael:

Greetings, Beloved – We are ready to speak to you and excited to inform you that this part of the process is over! We would still like you to write every day as a regular outlet of thoughts and ideas – please adjust your thinking accordingly, for We know that your expectations have been to write solely for the book's sake. This was a good beginning and suitable for creating an illumined manuscript, but as you realized a moment ago, these Transmissions also act as a reminder of your Divine connection and as a source of information about your personal growth as well. Such it is with all things – there are many layers of meaning and usefulness, which is why such appeals to you – indeed, has always appealed to you. Things that do "double duty"!

Go and see Lelon – and write again tonight. We love you and are so proud of you!

MARCH 6, 2016
AM, HOME

Archangel Michael:

Good morning, Beloved – We feel your stress and excitement about the many things you have yet to do, and We promise that you have help – lots of help! – to complete everything easily. Do not worry; you are always supported and protected.

(Sorry, Beloved, your attention wandered, and you couldn't hear Us for a moment. But now we are all back on the same frequency.)

You were thinking yesterday about teleporting, and it feels similar to the frequency shift you just experienced. And no, it's not "harder" to jump one room over than to jump to Paris. You are in a phase where you are learning to recognize places and people by their "feel," and it is this skill you will use when you bi-locate. Yesterday also you watched television and thought how you'd dislike living in the city depicted on screen. That city had a frequency, as does the place you live now. You will simply embody that frequency and "snap" there. Truthfully, you've done this before, so it won't be a complete surprise, although the novelty will remain awhile.

We feel you wondering about the mechanics – can you take your purse, your car, other people? You can go as you are – taking with you whatever you intend. In other words, your clothes, shoes, purse; all will of course go with you. You can take a car, or a chair, or a suitcase, but you will soon learn that you need none of them. As for taking another person, no, you cannot. Each must be at the right frequency to bi-locate. In the specific case of your mother, yes, you could "jump" her to the new location, but she is already at a frequency where she could do this for herself; it would be like a driving instructor in the car with a student driver. Cats astral travel all the time, so the cats could go, too, but they would prefer to travel using their own gifts.

You are also wondering about the television show you saw last night about psychopaths. These humans have only two strands of DNA turned on, and the process has not yet completed for the rest of their DNA strands to be plugged in. These unfortunate Souls are remnants of the time when all humans' DNA was unplugged. Yes, they came through the upgrade in the 1940s that plugged in all thirteen strands, but as always, there is a curve, and the people at the bottom end of the curve experience things more slowly. They are constantly beamed Light to try and lift them, but they must accept the Light, and it is their free will to accept, or not to accept. There is also a difference between people who are true "psychopaths," i.e. those whose DNA is literally unplugged, and those who use their free will to do horrible things, although "being unplugged" does certainly make it easier to do horrible things (what are *perceived* to be horrible things – remember, there is no judgment of experiences here). The population in your prisons (globally) are largely these "unplugged" humans – they exist largely by instinct and they are incapable of much more than breeding and eating. Their connection to Source has been intentionally suppressed. It may be helpful if you go back and reread the section on DNA, Beloved.

One final thing, before we go; yes, the breakout on your face is related to the candy you ate last night. Please allow us to continue the upgrades – and sugar, a metabolic destabilizer – causes the changes to fluctuate, and settle into solidity much slower. In other words, your diet is holding you back in a very literal way. Please be mindful of this.

MARCH 12, 2016
AM, HOME

Archangel Michael:

Good morning, Beloved – We are so glad that you heard our Message to take care of yourself first – and listened to it! This is what the Dalai Lama would call "wise selfish." You must take time to do what matters most for yourself, so you have the energy and excitement to pursue Our (and your) mission. We believe your photos turned out very well, and We are proud of you for taking them. And yes, you heard us correctly – the ones where you don't like the way you look are your *perception* of yourself, but the Photoshopped one is how you really are. Very soon now that will also be your own perception, and it will become "real." (You understand We say "real" because it already is real, but, as you would say, it hasn't filtered down to 3D yet.) Continue to purge and divest yourself of residual self-image; that's not you anymore, and in fact, *it never was.* People have always seen you as Lelon described; why do you think they always want to be around you? They feel better! But you must take an action, Beloved, to strengthen your bubble – it has some holes which people exploit, after which you feel tired and drained. This is a one-time action – you are correct in that you don't have to repeatedly ask for what you want. The "new way" is to ask in expectancy of receiving (whatever), and then detach from the timing and outcome and just receive. So, the action is to sit back; do it now and record it later.

You are already very adept at grounding – and your mental image of closing all the computer windows is very apt. What We did is to guide you to restart your Merkaba (which you first consciously spun during the Flower of Life workshop) (see Appendix E) in such a way that you could set the switch to "auto" – it will spin in "protection" mode almost constantly, i.e. every time someone tries to take energy without your permission. We also had you set the switch to "protection" mode rather than "travel" mode, although that feature is now available! So, here's how the protection grid works: anybody out in the environment who simply wants free food (energy) cannot now use you as a source. But, people with whom you have contracts can still get in, so finish up those lessons and allow those tiny holes to seal!

Enough for now. We will speak again.

Michele:

I dreamt last night of two infants, one large one and one small one. Archangels, what does this mean?

Archangel Michael:

The larger dream child is your budding relationship with reconnected friends. The smaller dream child, the one you were cuddling and tickling under the chin and cooing to, is this book. It is born and its life cycle begins!

MARCH 14, 2016
EARLY AM, HOME

Archangel Michael:

All your hard work is paying off, Beloved – soon the event will be successfully concluded, and it will be wonderful – people will flock to it as they flock wherever you are! (No, it is no coincidence that restaurants and stores fill up when you go in them; others feel your energy pull and are attracted there.)

Soon we will impulse you to begin typing the book, and then an opportunity for publishing will appear. You don't need to worry, for We promised you We will handle everything, and We will. The dream you had – where you went with your mother and others into a trash-filled compound, with people living in industrial spaces, and everyone afraid – is partially a mish-mash of the television you watched last night and partially an image of the future. The conservative, political, religious, educational, class-oriented society you live in is but a superficial skin, and what a person truly *is* lies beneath it!

Soon your own Twin Flame will appear – We know you think about him, and worry that he will be argumentative, and will cheat, and will abandon you eventually (as others have) – but, Beloved, you must believe Us when We say that higher relationships are different than 3D ones. When there are no more lessons to learn, no more contracts to complete, no more karmic relationships and situations to resolve, two people can just *be* – as you will be with your own Beloved. He will adore you and treat you like the Queen you are. Lelon's Twin Flame approaches as well, We are pleased to report. And yes, his [cat] Claire is definitely back as a "walk-in" in that body. So Lelon will see Claire again in this "lifetime." (We are so pleased to see you now feel as strangely as We do, using words like "this time," and "later" and "truthfully"!)

Go and prepare for your day. It will be a good one!

MARCH 26, 2016
AM, HOME

Archangel Michael:

Hello, Beloved, We have missed speaking with you! It would be of great benefit for you and us to speak daily – the book is but one facet of the relationship We have.

You dreamed of Paris because you will soon be there yourself – this is part of the amazing life you live, although you often fail to perceive its wonder. So many of your fellow Earth citizens have never been beyond their own home cities or home states, yet you have traveled the globe! You were attracted to [Elizabeth Gilbert's novel] *Eat, Pray, Love* because this is also your life path – to travel, eat, write, and pray (that is, to fulfill your mission of compassionately helping others to Awaken). "Pray" has a bad connotation for many who feel that Church has become corrupted, but prayer is one of the most powerful forces on your Earth. It is the Universe in alignment and it is instantaneous manifestation. Simply sitting in reflective space and asking for the best outcome for all – this is true prayer. Your many friends pray for you daily, among them Maddie and Lelon. They love you so much! Your well-being is being guarded and your hopes and dreams are being brought to reality by the legions of Light Beings and Light Warriors on this world and in all Realms. Your mission is critical – you must begin to put yourself, and your mission, first! You recently read a message about warning signs from the Universe – these are true. We prefer to see them as signposts, but when the person in question is mired in low energy, a "warning" is appropriate. Remember your analogy of a [lessons coming lightly at first, like a] pebble, [and if ignored, then as] a rock, and [if still ignored, finally as a thrown] brick? Just so. Some people require a brick to Awaken!

This is not to say that the "work" you do isn't worthwhile – since it's not a brick! – but rather that you in particular, Beloved, tend to be 100 percent. Either/or. Black or white. Work or play. There is a lovely balance, Beloved, and you must find yours. We urge you to write and speak to Us daily, eat better, and get up at 5:30 AM. See if life improves, little scientist!

We love you so much – be well and enjoy your father and stepmother today!

MARCH 27, 2016
AM, HOME

Archangel Michael:

The discomfort you feel this morning is the remnants of the old way leaving your system. No longer is there 3D or even 4D left within your psyche or auric field. In a very short time these changes will anchor in your physical body and you will feel so much better – so many lingering issues will simply disappear, among them the headaches and stomach problems (bloating, gas, quick blood pressure). This is quite important for you to remember, Beloved – the issues are *gone.* We emphasize this because from now on, any symptoms you manifest – whether these or others – will be *signposts.* They will guide you in the direction of your mission. When you are calm and "on the right path" things will flow. When things bog down, you will instantly know to go in another direction. Your dream of graduating from high school was indeed a prescient one – you have graduated today out of 3D and into 5D. Congratulations! The hard work – and although you now know it needn't have been quite so hard – was a completion of all the past experiences and traumas, a true clearing, preparing your Vessel for the upcoming fun (We cannot call it "work," so we call it "fun"!). Keep writing. Keep using your pendulum. Find ways to create balance – for no longer is it best to work, work, work until exhaustion. Everything in moderation, Beloved. That is all.

APRIL 19, 2016
AM, HOME

Archangel Michael:

Good morning, Beloved One – remember, your only mission here is to raise the vibration in the space around you – to feel good about being here today and to indeed manifest the Eagle Eye perspective!

APRIL 25, 2016
PM, HOME

Archangel Michael:

Ah, Beloved, We salute your decision to begin breathing again! You heard us correctly when We likened writing to breathing in your case. Next you must trust that an early start will improve your mood, your allergies, and even your skin. Everything is as it should be, although you are using your fee will to create an outcome that is not all that you would wish.

The dream of the locusts – it was a sign to jump into the writing with "all your feet" and trust the wind to carry you safely. Too, you are in a group of like-minded and like-missioned people whose job it is to scrub clean the face of the Earth; the "Spiritual Warriors" Lelon speaks of.

Now, Beloved, it is time. You must arise when We awaken you with our Beloved [cat] Geoffrey and write. Your dream is right around the corner – leap and the net will appear!

APRIL 26, 2016
PM, HOME

Archangel Michael:

What visions came into your head this night, Beloved? We send you a combination of fruit and locusts, of famine and fabulous. We know this does not appear to make any sense now, but We promise you, it will!

(a different voice smoothly takes over)

There is so much We wish to say to you now that you are writing again – that you speak with Us daily is a great joy, a treasure, and a great pleasure for Us. We do so love to express Ourselves in written form! The letters flow across the page like a river, like a lambent stream of glittering scales. Clearly, this is a poet speaking, as usually Archangel Michael is not so flowing in his language. In fact, tonight you speak with Me, the Archangel Gabriel, the Archangel of communication – the master of language in all its many forms, colors, and textures, and Master of Music. Music... the language of the stars, the language of Love. We come to you full of effusive praise for your sincere willingness to flow from the pen, to create a jewel-bright masterpiece in written form, a magnificent manifesto of Kindness and Compassion. We love this, and We love you! Do you see? – *yes, you do see!* – how different Our language is! Our unique Spirits that encase our meanings, cloaking them in layers of divinity and excellence? It is not enough to say, "It is good." You must opine: *"The flavors were excellently presented in splendid combinations to create the exquisite and never-before-tasted flavor explosion that drenched my mouth in savory juices."* I, the Archangel Gabriel, have made My way through to your pen to give you such phrasing. Archangel Michael will supply the "meat" and I, the Archangel Gabriel, will supply the "seasoning"! Then [your guide] Archimedes will reduce the dish to its ultimate perfection. Thus it shall be. We will speak again!

MAY 11, 2016
PM, Home

Archangel Michael:

Epiphany! Beloved has discovered that her opinions and ideas matter more than others', even others' whom she loves! We rejoice with you over this small piece of Heaven, this revelation that was so self-evident that finally, Beloved knows, she has integrated this piece of wisdom – she has assimilated its meaning and has come out the other side.

Your friend Fred had much to say on the topic of being a published author, and he was divinely inspired to share [author Stuart Pressfield's] *The War of Art* with you, Beloved; you needed to know the blockage was not a character fault or lack of willpower. The discussion, too, of the role of the Dark (yin, evil, low) to slow down the process and keep it in Divine Right Timing was both timely and apt. There is so much to say about the role of the Dark! The beings who agreed to come here and play dark roles are most worthy (although you know We do not hold to such delineations as "worthy" or "not worthy") of Compassion, Beloved. It is easy to love, and to find the Love within, those beings who are pleasant and helpful, who assist you willingly with your mission. It is much harder to feel compassion for the others – where, truly, the real lessons and wisdom lie – because sometimes the sliver of Light is so slight you must hunt for it with true diligence (image of looking into a microscope). Your Dalai Lama said enemies are the best teachers, and this highly enlightened being is a wise master for Earth at this time. He is a being high in the Light and has managed to remain remarkably humble because he knows and lives his mission constantly. He is here to show an example of Love and Light to all with eyes to see and ears to hear. Is it not wonderful how everything falls so neatly together with all your reading and information neatly dovetailing (We love this word!) one into the other?

Archangel Gabriel wishes to say something about the Dark and its role:

Archangel Gabriel:

Thus it has always been since the Beginning: when, with Creator, We [the Archangels] Co-created the seven Universes and set the Gods to rule over them – that each part shall have its mate, and never alone, complete and perfect Unity to balance a world (or a Universe) on the cosmic scale of justice and harmony – a perfect blend of the Light and Dark, up and down, male and female. Each using its Heavenly influence to grow and stretch the very fabric of the Universe (space/time) to allow for new experiences in the Celestial Heaven that humans call "Earth"! For what could you know of Light unless you had also seen darkness? How would you know sweet, if sour had not been experienced? How could plants survive without both sun and rain?

So, We impart to you the dancing vision of Ultimate Wisdom: the Dark serves a purpose – to "check" the Light and to prevent unlimited growth. For too much of any one thing is not in balance. The Universe must balance. Thus will Darkness remain, as a powerful force in its own right and as a necessary and beloved aspect of the created Universe. But more wisdom is at hand – a just and balanced Universe is not necessarily an *equal* Universe. Just as a teaspoon of salt "goes a long way," a pinch of darkness will serve to slow down the Light as much as necessary. The forces of Light and Dark struggle at fifty/fifty, and they struggle at ninety/ten, for even 10 percent dark is efficient enough to produce the necessary amount of slowing-down, of wait-and-see, to accomplish all that is required.

You have done beautifully this morning, Vessel – We applaud you. If you are still tired, you may rest again. We love you!

MAY 12, 2016
PM, HOME

Archangel Michael:

We are glad to see and feel your delight, Beloved One. We told you to make this simple change to help you see the real effects of following the path – it can be a pleasant stroll through the woods or a hard slog up a rocky pathway. Either way will get you to where you're going, but some ways are more enjoyable than others! As always, your free will allows you to choose. (Remember, too, that your free will also allows you to choose again.)

Sleep now, and we will speak in the morning early. You have a download and an upgrade scheduled for tonight, but We will ensure you sleep well and wake up rested. Pleasant evening to you!

End of Book One

GLOSSARY

Akash, or Akashic Records – A compendium of thoughts, feelings, events, and emotions encoded within the non-physical astral plane; they contain the energetic records of all souls about their past lives, the present lives, and possible future lives. Each soul has its own Akashic Records, like a series of "books," with each "book" representing one lifetime. Within that book/lifetime is recorded a person's entire history, including feelings, thoughts, decisions, lessons, outcomes, learnings, and possibilities. The Hall (or Library) of the Akashic Records is where all souls' Akashic Records are stored energetically. In other words, the information is stored in the Akashic field (also called zero point field). The Akashic Records contain the collective wisdom of all sentient beings and are available as a resource to those beings. (adapted from Wikipedia and www.akashicrecordsofsouls.com)

Babaji, or Mahavatar Babaji – Great spiritual teacher from India in the tradition of Jesus Christ, Quan Yin, Buddha, and others. (see Quan Yin)

Bi-location – Celestial term for teleportation, the process of moving from one place to another instantaneously and without the use of technology (such as a car or airplane). Distinct from astral travel in that the corporeal body is also transported, not just the ethereal body.

Chakra – Centers of energy in the human body, generally considered to be located along the midline of the body. Depending on the system, there are between 7-15 chakras. The most commonly known are these seven: crown (7th, violet, located one hand-width above the top of the head), brow/third eye/pineal (6th, indigo, located in center of the forehead), throat (5th, blue, behind the Adam's apple), heart (4th, green, center of the chest), solar plexus (3rd, yellow, mid-abdomen, just below ribcage), sacral/navel (2nd, orange, three finger-widths below the navel), and the root (1st, red, one hand-width below the perineum). Some systems add an additional chakra between the throat and heart, called the high heart chakra. It then becomes the 4th chakra, the color of which is sky blue, and it is located roughly in the notch at the base of the throat. Body energy runs through these chakras, and if that energy is blocked, illness can occur. Reiki and other energy healing methods can unblock the energy and promote healing. (adapted from www.chopra.com)

Channel - Channeling (or Channelling) is the process of communicating with any consciousness that is not in physical human form by allowing that consciousness to express itself through an individual, the Channeler [or in Michele's case, the "Vessel"]. Channeling usually refers to accessing higher knowledge to support spiritual growth and to gain greater clarity about one's life. It is a method used to access information from entities that are more evolved and can therefore enlighten us as we move through the evolution of consciousness and back to Source. (adapted from www.spiritlibrary.com)

Codes – Specific genes, selected during the Interlife review process, to "switch on" (or to remain off) depending on the lessons or activities chosen for that lifetime. For example, if a woman chooses during the Interlife to experience the next lifetime without having children, the codes allowing a pregnancy will remain in the "off" position.

Deresolve, or derez – To dematerialize at the atomic level; to return to source energy. When a Soul leaves the incarnate body upon "death," one option is to dereolve the body and pack it into electronic storage for later use (at which time the body would rematerialize).

Divine Feminine – Represents the connection to the part of your consciousness responsible for inward retrospection, nurture, intuition, and empathy, regardless of your gender; the aspect of the self associated with creation, intuition, community, sensuality ("felt" sense rather than "thinking" sense), and collaboration. (adapted from www.SuzanneKingsbury.net) (See Appendix F)

Divine Masculine – Regardless of your gender, represents the connection to the part of your consciousness responsible for outward direction, logical action toward a goal, thinking, and making judgments about situations and consequences. It is the aspect of self associated with thinking, competition, calculation, and rationality. (See Appendix F)

Draconians – Sentient humanoid reptilian beings usually associated with the star system Draco. Green, blue, gray/brown skin with scales. Very high intelligence, but below-average emotional responses. (adapated from www.Gaia.com)

Energy – Literal translation is "air" or "breath;" concept is known in nearly every ancient culture and is widely acknowledged in Eastern countries. This energy is the "life force" which permeates the body and animates it; in Traditional Chinese Medicine, the "chi" is said to flow through specific meridians in the body, and manipulating these meridians can restore or improve health. Also called "qi" in Chinese languages; "gi" in Korea; "ki" or "chi" in Japan; "prana" in Hindu traditions; "mana" in Hawaiian cultures; "manitou" in the Native American cultures; "ruah" in Jewish culture; and "vital energy" in Western philosophy. (adapted from Wikipedia)

Frequency, *see vibration*

Gaia – The sentient being that is the Soul of the physical incarnation of planet Earth.

Galactic Council or Galactic Federation – The Galactic Federation of Worlds (or Galactic Council) is a large federation of civilizations from many different planets, galaxies and universes working together for the harmonious existence of all life. There is a galactic federation in each of the inhabited galaxies of our universe. These federations are part of the universal management structure much like field offices are part of the management structure for a large corporation. (adapted from www.NibiruanCouncil.com)

Greys – One of the most well-known humanoid alien species; short stature with grey skin and large dark eyes. Commonly referred to in sightings of UFOs, extraterrestrials, and "alien abduction" scenarios.

Hue-man – Celestial term for the ascended Beings we are becoming, as distinct from "humans," who are still in the process of ascension.

Interlife – A review and planning period between incarnations intended to allow Souls to assess lessons completed, lessons still to be learned, and to form contracts between all the "players" in a given lifetime.

Merkaba, or MerKaBa – Another name for one's Light Body. Part of full consciousness when spiritual, astral and physical bodies are integrated. The Merkaba allows Self to shrink to baseball size and to travel anywhere, instantly. *See Appendix E.*

Oversoul – An Oversoul allows for comprehensive experience in all directions and all timelines. Each Soul in a Soul cluster (or Soul group/family) is part of a larger aspect called an Oversoul. The Oversoul is like a cup of water dipped from the ocean, and each individual incarnation is a drop of water from the cup. All are the same source material, just temporarily "separated out" to experience a certain lesson, but ultimately returning to the ocean (the Universe). For example, Jesus, Babaji, Quan Yin, Buddha, and others were all part of the same Oversoul. (See Soul family)

Pineal gland – Pea-sized gland shaped like a pine cone located in the middle of the human brain. For Buddhists, the pineal is a symbol of spiritual awakening. In Hinduism, the pineal is the seat of intuition and clairvoyance. For Taoists, the pineal is the mind's eye or heavenly eye. In a spiritual context, the pineal gland is your "third eye," which acts as an antenna to receive higher-dimensional messages. (See Chakra) When open and receiving, an active pineal gland creates clarity and intuition, and psychic abilities are possible. (See Appendix C).

Quan Yin – Enlightened Soul sent to Earth to awaken humans in ancient Asia. (See Babaji)

Reincarnation – Belief that after physical death, the same Soul returns in a different body to continue or expand on lessons or experiences of previous lifetimes.

Schumann Resonance – Global electromagnetic resonances in the Earth's low-frequency spectrum. Often called the "heartbeat" of Earth, these frequencies have been steady around 7.83 Hertz for as long as humans have been keeping records. Recent spikes may indicate that the "heartbeat" is speeding up – that the frequency is increasing. (For more information, visit https://lifeshaping.me/blog/category/understanding-the-schumann-resonance-and-its-effect-on-you)

Sirians – Race of feline/leonine humanoids from the star system Sirius. These mathematically-minded scientists are master geneticists and engineers and are responsible for creating the original Earth human's physical vehicles (bodies).

Soul family (Soul cluster, Soul group) – Group/cluster of people who are all from the same Heavenly family, who agree to incarnate and learn lessons together. May or may not be what we think of as "real" (biological) family. (See Tribe)

Soul mate – People on the same Soul journey; people who enter your life for a reason, a season, or a lifetime. They may be members of your Soul Group/Soul Family/Tribe. A person with whom you have a pre-arrangement to learn a Soul lesson. (also "Soulmate")

Star beings – General term for sentient beings from other planets, galaxies, or universes. (Examples: Sirians, Draconians, Andromedeans, etc.)

Synchronicity – A seemingly-magical (or seemingly-coincidental) coming together of people, places, and things to create a miraculous outcome.

Tribe – A group of individuals here on Earth to learn a lesson together; an organic, constantly-changing web of interconnected Souls. Your tribe is made up of those you choose to connect with to share your life, your triumphs, and your challenges. May include friends, family, co-workers, pets, Nature, fellow congregants in a house of faith, etc.

Twin Flame – a special kind of Soul mate who is a lifelong partner, usually husband or wife (sometimes brother and sister or parent and child). Some traditions suggest that a Twin Flame is literally the "other half" or "matching partner" of your own Soul.

Vibration – the rate of speed at which something moves; the higher the vibration rate (or frequency), the faster something moves; the lower the vibration rate, the slower. As beings ascend, their frequency rises, until the molecules move apart enough for physical changes to occur (such as bi-location, spontaneous healing, etc.).

APPENDIX A

Drunvalo Melchizedek - The Meaning of In Lak'ech
by Gregg Prescott, M.S.
Editor, In5D.com

Drunvalo Melchizedek explains the meaning of "In Lak'ech" and how the Mayan culture used this terminology with one another.

Have you ever heard anyone say "In Lak'ech" or "In Lak'ech Ala K'in"?

Sometimes you'll see it spelled this way: "In lak'esh" but the correct spelling is "In Lak'ech". "In Lak'ech Ala K'in" means *"you are another me"* or *"I am another you."* The traditional Mayan interpretation simply means *"I am you. You are me."*

This is very similar to the West India origin of "Namaste" which has a variety of definitions generally meaning "I bow to you," "reverence to you," or "the light in me honors the light in you."

The Lakota have a saying amongst their culture: "Mitakuye Oyasin," which means "We are all related," but can also be used in warfare. According to one Lakota website, "Only Lakota can use this word as it is in our language." It is spoken during prayer and ceremony to invite and acknowledge all relatives to the moment.

In Lak'ech Ala K'in is not just a statement that we say to one another. It can be said to greet the morning sun, for the appreciation and gratitude of water or any other element or sentient being on this planet.

http://in5d.com/drunvalo-melchizedek-the-meaning-of-in-lakech/

APPENDIX B

Spiritual Meaning of Numbers

Here are Drunvalo Melchizedek's list of triple numbers and their meanings from pages 88-89 of his book *The Serpent of Light: Beyond 2012:*

- 111 - Energy Flow: Any energy flow such as electricity, money, water, sexual energy, etc.
- 222 - New Cycle: The beginning of a new cycle, the nature of which depends on the next triple number you see.
- 333 - Decision: You have a decision to make. The decision will lead to either 666, which means you must repeat the lesson again in some other way, or it will lead to 999, which is completion and you have learned the lesson.
- 444 - The Mystery School: What is occurring in life is a lesson around learning about the Reality. This school is learning, such as reading books or studying a subject, but not actual doing.
- 555 - Unity Consciousness: This is the number when someone has attained Unity Consciousness. They have mastered all levels of the Mystery School. It is the highest number. It is the number of Christ.
- 666 - Earth Consciousness: This is the number of the Beast in the Bible, so it can represent pure evil, but it is also the number of mankind and life. Carbon is the basis of life, and carbon has six protons, six neutrons, and six electrons. Generally, when you see this number, it means to watch out for physical events that are presenting themselves at that moment, and you must be careful.
- 777 - The Mystery School: This is the part of the school where you are not just reading books about life but are also practicing it.
- 888 - Completion of a particular lesson within the Mystery School.
- 999 - Completion of a particular cycle of events.
- 000 - Has no value.

Alternative Meanings to Triple Numbers (In Light Times... A Metaphysical, Spiritual, Holistic Publication
Copyright © 1998, 1999, 2000, 2001, 2002, 2003, 2004 - In Light Times - ALL RIGHTS RESERVED November 1999. www.inlightimes.com):

Long ago, the Angels taught me that when you see a triple number in the Reality, it has significance relative to what you are thinking or the environment around you. It has to do with music and the fact that all notes in an octave separate themselves by eleven cycles per second. Therefore, the separations of each note to each other are 11, 22, 33, 44, 55, 66, 77, 88, and 99 cycles per second, or multiples of these numbers, which presents a perfectly harmonic tuning or moment in time, since the entire Reality was created through the harmonics of music.

Therefore, when triple numbers or more appear, in any manner, it physically represents a mathematical moment in time that contains the harmonics of the value of that number. In human words, 444 would best be described as the Mystery School, which is where one learns about the Reality.

Here are alternative meanings to the appearance of triple numbers:

- 111 — Monitor your thoughts carefully and be sure to only think about what you want, not what you don't want. This sequence is a sign that there is a gate of opportunity opening, and your thoughts are manifesting into form at record speeds. The 111 is like the bright light of a flash bulb. It means the universe has just taken a snapshot of your thoughts and is manifesting them into form. Are you pleased with what thoughts the universe has captured? If not, correct your thoughts (ask your angels to help you with this if you have difficulty controlling or monitoring your thoughts).
- 222 — Our newly planted ideas are beginning to grow into reality. Keep watering and nurturing them, and soon they will push through the soil so you can see evidence of your manifestation. In other words, don't quit five minutes before the miracle. Your manifestation is soon going to be evident to you, so keep up the good work! Keep holding positive thoughts, keep affirming, and continue visualizing.
- 333 — The Ascended Masters are near you, desiring you to know that you have their help, love, and companionship. Call upon the Ascended Masters often, especially when you see the number 3 patterns around you. Some of the more famous Ascended Masters include Jesus, Moses, Mary, Quan Yin, and Yogananda.
- 444 — The angels are surrounding you now, reassuring you of their love and help. Don't worry because the angels' help is nearby.
- 555 — Buckle your seatbelts. A major life change is upon you. This change should not be viewed as being "positive" or "negative," since all change is but a natural part of life's flow. Perhaps this change is an answer to your prayers, so continue seeing and feeling yourself being at peace.

- 666 — Your thoughts are out of balance right now, focused too much on the material world. This number sequence asks you to balance your thoughts between heaven and earth. Like the famous "Sermon on the Mount," the angels ask you to focus on spirit and service and know your material and emotional needs will automatically be met as a result.
- 777 — The angels applaud you... congratulations, you're on a roll! Keep up the good work and know your wish is coming true. This is an extremely positive sign and means you should also expect more miracles to occur.
- 888 — A phase of your life is about to end, and this is a sign to give you forewarning to prepare. This number sequence may mean you are winding up an emotional career, or relationship phase. It also means there is light at the end of the tunnel. In addition, it means, "The crops are ripe. Don't wait to pick and enjoy them." In other words, don't procrastinate making your move or enjoying fruits of your labor.
- 999 — Completion. This is the end of a big phase in your personal or global life. Also, it is a message to lightworkers involved in Earth healing and means "Get to work because Mother Earth needs you right now."
- 000 — A reminder you are one with God, and to feel the presence of your Creator's love within you. Also, it is a sign that a situation has gone full circle.

APPENDIX C

Each section adapted from Wikipedia page of that title

ESP: According to Wikipedia, extrasensory perception, or ESP, "also called **sixth sense**, includes reception of information not gained through the recognized physical senses but sensed with the mind. The term was adopted by Duke University psychologist J. B. Rhine to denote psychic abilities such as telepathy, clairaudience, and clairvoyance, and their trans-temporal operation as precognition or retrocognition. The words "clairvoyance" and "psychic" are often used to refer to many different kinds of paranormal sensory experiences, but there are more specific names:

Clairsentience (feeling/touching)
Clairsentience is a form of extra-sensory perception wherein a person acquires psychic knowledge primarily by feeling.[52] The word "clair" is French for "clear", and "sentience" is derived from the Latin sentire, "to feel". Psychometry is related to clairsentience. The word stems from *psyche* and *metric*, which means "soul-measuring."

Clairaudience (hearing/listening)
In the field of parapsychology, **clairaudience** [from late 17th century French *clair* (clear) and audience (hearing)] is a form of extra-sensory perception wherein a person acquires information by paranormal auditory means. It is often considered to be a form of clairvoyance. Clairaudience is essentially the ability to hear in a paranormal manner, as opposed to paranormal seeing (clairvoyance) and feeling (clairsentience).

Clairalience (smelling)
Also known as **clairescence.** In the field of parapsychology, **clairalience** (or alternatively, **clairolfactance**) [presumably from late 17th century French *clair* (clear) and alience (smelling)] is a form of extra-sensory perception wherein a person accesses psychic knowledge through the physical sense of smell.

Claircognizance (knowing)
In the field of parapsychology, **claircognizance** [presumably from late 17th century French *clair* (clear) and *cognizance* (knowledge)] is a form of extra-sensory perception wherein a person acquires psychic knowledge primarily by means of intrinsic knowledge. It is the ability to know something without a physical explanation why you know it, like the concept of mediums.

Clairgustance (tasting)
In the field of parapsychology, **clairgustance** is defined as a form of extra-sensory perception that allegedly allows one to taste a substance without putting anything in one's mouth. It is claimed that those who possess this ability are able to perceive the essence of a substance from the spiritual or ethereal realms through taste.

Clairenunciate (communicate)
Speak fluently in metaphors and creative in conjoining context.

APPENDIX D

Sacred Geometry and the Flower of Life
From www.crystalinks.com/sg.html and http://www.crystalinks.com/floweroflife.html
(article reprinted with permission)

Sacred geometry involves sacred universal patterns used in the design of everything in our reality, most often seen in sacred architecture and sacred art. The basic belief is that geometry and mathematical ratios, harmonics and proportion are also found in music, light, cosmology. This value system is seen as widespread even in prehistory, a cultural universal of the human condition.

It is considered foundational to building sacred structures such as temples, mosques, megaliths, monuments and churches; sacred spaces such as altars, temenoi and tabernacles; meeting places such as sacred groves, village greens and holy wells and the creation of religious art, iconography and using "divine" proportions. Alternatively, sacred geometry-based arts may be ephemeral, such as visualization, sand painting and medicine wheels.

Sacred geometry may be understood as a worldview of pattern recognition, a complex system of religious symbols and structures involving space, time and form. According to this view the basic patterns of existence are perceived as sacred. By connecting with these, a believer contemplates the Great Mysteries, and the Great Design. By studying the nature of these patterns, forms and relationships and their connections, insight may be gained into the mysteries – the laws and lore of the Universe.

In ancient civilizations, the golden ratio (sacred geometry) was often employed in the design of art and architecture - from the simple spiral to more complex designs. Today sacred geometry is still used in the planning and construction of many structures such as churches, temples, mosques, religious monuments, altars, tabernacles, sacred spaces and the creation of religious art.

The Flower of Life is the modern name given to a geometrical figure composed of multiple evenly spaced, overlapping circles, that are arranged so that they form a flower-like pattern with a six-fold symmetry like a hexagon. The center of each circle is on the circumference of six surrounding circles of the same diameter.

It is considered by some to be a symbol of sacred geometry, said to contain ancient, religious value depicting the fundamental forms of space and time. In this sense, it is a visual expression of the connections life weaves through all sentient beings, believed to contain a type of Akashic Record of basic information of all living things.

There are many spiritual beliefs associated with the Flower of Life; for example, depictions of the five Platonic Solids are found within the symbol of Metatron's Cube, which may be derived from the Flower of Life pattern. These platonic solids are geometrical forms which are said to act as a template from which all life springs.

Another notable example of that which may be derived from the Flower of Life is the Tree of Life. This has been an important symbol of sacred geometry for many people from various religious backgrounds. Particularly, the teachings of the Kabbalah have dealt intricately with the Tree of Life.

According to Drunvalo Melchizedek, in the Judeo-Christian tradition, the stages which construct the Seed of Life are said to represent the seven days of Creation, in which Elohim (God/concept of divinity) created life; Genesis 2:2–3, Exodus 23:12, 31:16–17, Isaiah 56:6–8. Within these stages, among other things, are the symbols of the Vesica Piscis (an ancient religious symbol) and Borromean rings (which represents the Holy Trinity).

Melchizedek, Drunvalo. *The Ancient Secret of the Flower of Life, Volume I.*
Melchizedek, Drunvalo. *The Ancient Secret of the Flower of Life, Volume II.*

APPENDIX E

Merkaba or Mer-Ka-Ba
(article used with permission)

Merkaba is another name for one's Light Body. Part of full consciousness, when spiritual, astral and physical bodies are integrated. The Merkaba allows self to shrink to baseball size and to travel anywhere, instantly.

The MerKaBa is a spinning structure of light similar to the **chakras**. It is similar in that when spinning properly it works as an inter-dimensional gateway – kind of a **Star Gate** – so that higher consciousness may incarnate into the physical body. The difference is that the MerKaBa is much larger, encompassing the entire body. In fact, the MerKaBa is the structure of spinning light which allows for the incarnation of the Light body itself. Without the MerKaBa being activated the other parts of the Light body such as the Chakras cannot incarnate properly and may not be stable.

When the MerKaBa is activated it forms a counter-rotating field of spiritual light which creates a dimensional gateway for the Light body to stabilize within the physical body and for its other structures such as the Chakra's to activate and stabilize as well. This allows for the possibility of incarnating higher consciousness permanently as well as raising the vibration of the physical body.

You will be also aligned to your Higher Self and Monad. If you successfully activate the Merkaba, it becomes possible to take the physical body into the fourth dimension. In Hebrew MerKaBa is spelt MerKaVa which means Chariot and indeed that's exactly what it is. It is a vehicle which can take you and your body between dimensions. Once raised into the fourth dimension the physical body will become much more subtle and may live for much longer. The possibility is also there to rise into even higher dimensions. This is where multidimensional, spiritual Healing takes place.

When the MerKaBa spins at a certain speed, a disk of light shoots out from the base Chakra, in the perfect center of the spinning star tetrahedron, to around 50-60 feet in diameter. This field of light has an electro-magnetic component that can be seen with the appropriate instruments on a computer monitor.

APPENDIX F

Divine Feminine and Divine Masculine

Historically, human cultures already know how to value the active principles associated with the Divine Masculine: sunshine; harvest; hunting; labor and activity; using the five senses to explore and explain the world around us; using the logical, left-brain to find solutions to problems and "take charge" to "make a difference." Wonderful masculinity! We could not exist without Divine Masculine ensuring that crops get planted, the books balance, and the laws are written down. The "yang" is easy to understand and appreciate.

Along the way, humans lost some of their appreciation for the Divine Feminine, the "yin" or passive and receptive quality that tempers movement. Divine Feminine is about using the abstract, right brain to allow community to develop and thrive; to sit and patiently and wait for the plants to mature and not pick them too soon; the creativity that spawns poetry, and paintings, and great sonatas; the darkness of night that allows rest and rejuvenation, and ultimately, wholeness.

Both aspects are needed for a balanced life and for a healthy culture (society, religion, politics, history/herstory, science, commerce) that supports and honors all members.

As Vikki Hanchen, MSW, states in her excellent article about Divine Masculine and Divine Feminine:

"In values of daily living, [honoring both Divine Feminine and Divine Masculine means] welcoming, including and listening to one another, in the service of understanding. It means affirming and supporting one another and seeking the unique gifts that each individual has to offer. It means accepting and respecting differences. It means being slow to judge, and open to compassion. It means being grounded in the heart, using the head in the service of the greater good. It means including intuition in perceiving and decision making. It means being connected to the goodness, aliveness, sensuality and wisdom of the body. It means using personal power to serve and to create, not to dominate and exploit."

STUFF I LOVE, (AKA ADDITIONAL RESOURCES)

BOOKS:

Beck, Martha. Finding Your Way in a Wild, New World: Reclaim Your True Nature to Create the Life You Want.

Braden, Gregg. *Resilience from the Heart: The Power to Thrive in Life's Extremes*

Braden, Gregg. *The Divine Matrix: Bridging Time, Space, Miracles, and Belief*

Braden, Gregg. *Fractal Time: The Secret of 2012 and a New World Age*

Carey, Ken. *The Starseed Transmissions.*

Cayce, Edgar. *My Life as a Seer.*

Crichton, Michael. *Travels.*

Dyer, Dr. Wayne. *There's A Spiritual Solution to Every Problem.*

Frissell, Bob. *Nothing in this Book Is True, But It's Exactly How Things Are.*

Gilbert, Elizabeth. *Eat, Pray, Love.*

Hay, Louise. *Heal Your Body: The Mental Causes for Physical Illness and the Metaphysical Way to Overcome Them.*

Herbert, Frank. Dune Chronicles series

Kahn, Matt. *Whatever Arises, Love That.* 1st ed. Boulder, Colorado: Sounds True Press, 2016.

LaFlamme, Jenna. *Pleasurable Weight Loss* (S&S, 2011)

Marciniak, Barbara. *Bringers of the Dawn.*

Marciniak, Barbara. *Earth.*

Marciniak, Barbara. *Family of Light.*

Marciniak, Barbara. *Path of Empowerment.*

MacEowen, Frank. *The Celtic Way of Seeing: Meditations on the Irish Spirit Wheel.*

MacEowen, Frank. *The Mist-Filled Path.*

McGowan, Kathleen. Magdalene trilogy: *The Expected One, The Book of Love,* and *The Poet Prince.*

Melchizedek, Drunvalo. *The Ancient Secret of the Flower of Life, Volume I.*

Melchizedek, Drunvalo. *The Ancient Secret of the Flower of Life, Volume II.*

Melchizedek, Drunvalo. *Serpent of Light: Beyond 2012: The Movement of the Earth's Kundalini and the Rise of the Female Light.*

Pressfield, Stuart, *The War of Art.*

Ward, Suzie. *Matthew, Tell Me About Heaven.*

Ward, Suzie. *Revelations for a New Era.*

WEBSITES:

www.marthabeck.com

www.matthewbooks.com

http://www.geometrycode.com/sacred-geometry/

www.therme-erding.de

Melchizedek, Drunvalo's videos: www.drunvalo.net

Thompson, Lelon, Intuitive Counselor, www.lelon.us

Mayan calendar: www.mayanmajix.com

Kryon: www.kryon.com

In Light Times: www.inlightimes.com

www.truedivinenature.com and videos (YouTube Channel: True Divine Nature)

MUSIC:

Amethystium

ATB

Blank and Jones

Blue Stone

Brule'

Conjure One

Daft Punk

Delerium

Eastern Sun

Enigma

Ryan Farish

Joey Fehrenbach

Jens Gad

Mythos

Nordlight

Paul Oakenfold

Schiller

Ulrich Schnauss

Lindsey Stirling

Tangerine Dream

Tycho

Vangelis

The Wingmakers

ACKNOWLEDGMENTS

Sincere thanks the many people who helped me write this book! First, my wonderful mother, Dr. Fran Baker, who listened to everything and gave wonderful feedback, and for her lovely ink drawings behind the quotes; to Lelon Thompson, who has encouraged me from Day One; to Marsha Kelly, my friend and willing ear, who read early drafts and gave kind and thoughtful comments; and to the many people who read and commented on my book: Ayana Iyi, Dwayne Butler, Zoubir Tabout and Mark Steven Wann, Vanessa Watson, Rhonda Burton, Susanne Carver, Lynne Creager, Nedwan Winters, Aisha Barnes, Nina Ghaffari and Jeff Rudis, and Eddie Lusk and Roberto Duran Rodriguez. I love you all!

Special Thanks

To Dr. Joe Muscolino, who told me years ago the only thing I ever needed to know to fulfill this path: "Writers *write*. So, get up every day and just do it!"

To Carol, who did me the deep kindness of reflecting my own uncertainty back to me when she scolded me for *purporting* to channel Archangel Michael. If that hadn't made me so angry at the time, I never would have sat down in earnest to prove her wrong... and I never would have discovered *it was all real.* I love and miss you, Carol!

To my best friend since 1981, Tina Dill, for always believing in me 110%, especially when I didn't believe in myself. I remember the day I told her that I heard angelic voices and wrote down what they told me. I was going to publish a book, and "they" told me it was going to sell a lot of copies. I asked if she thought I was just crazy or what, and she said, "It doesn't sound to me like you're crazy... it sounds to me like you're *blessed.*"

To Zoubir Tabout and Mark Steven Wann, who listened when I read and were impressed (and asked for more!), and who further favored me by translating this book into French and offering legal advice.

To Dr. David Morgan, for being an amazing friend since 1988, and for agreeing to buy two copies of this book even before it was published.

INDEX

K

L

M

P

R

S

T

U

V

Printed in the United States
By Bookmasters